Breaking Sad

Breaking Sad

What to Say After Loss, What Not to Say, and When to Just Show Up

edited by

Shelly Fisher & Jennifer Jones

SHE WRITES PRESS

Published 2017
Printed in the United States of America
ISBN: 978-1-63152-242-0 pbk.
ISBN: 978-1-63152-243-7 ebk.
Library of Congress Control Number: 2017949351

Cover and interior design by Tabitha Lahr

For information, address:
She Writes Press
1563 Solano Ave #546
Berkeley, CA 94707

She Writes Press is a division of SparkPoint Studio, LLC.

To Stephanie Yen-Mun Liem Azar, who was so accomplished and helped more people in her twenty-six years than most do in a lifetime.

And

To Herbert Lotman, who remains my hero, my inspiration and whose memory I try to honor every single day.

They both live on in the hearts of so many.

—Shelly Fisher

Contents

Introduction

The idea for this book came to me on a day in 2013 as I stood beside a close friend just hours after the death of her twenty-six-year-old daughter, Stephanie. Five days earlier, Stephanie had celebrated her birthday and was a glowing newlywed of not even a month who was eagerly anticipating the conclusion of her medical school training. Despite her youth, Stephanie had already touched and helped more people than most people do in a long lifetime. Now . . . this. What could I or anyone else possibly say to ease the family's unfathomable pain? What could I or anyone else possibly do?

Twice before, I'd stood beside parents on the day of a child's death, a witness to the awkward ballet of distraught looks, too-tight hugs, and tear-choked words that attend shattering loss. Then, as now, I'd heard fumbling attempts to comfort that surely only deepened the pain of the bereaved—misaimed expressions of sympathy like, "They are in a better place," and "Thank goodness you have other children," and "I can't imagine how someone survives something like this."

I know what it is to be on the receiving end of words and gestures that, though well intended, feel more discomforting than soothing. In 2014, I lost my father, my heart, the sun in my family's solar system, right before my daughter's wedding. A month earlier, my aunt (his sister) had lost her daughter (my cousin) suddenly. In 2009, I experienced a different sort of grief when I was diagnosed with breast cancer. I remember the people who went mute because they couldn't think what to say. The people who looked at the floor, too uncomfortable to look me in the eye. The people who literally shied away from me. The people who gave me the pitying "look."

For those who are grieving, well-wishers' responses can weigh still heavier as the months pass. In other people's eyes, they find, they are often reduced to "the one who had cancer" or "the widow" or "the people who lost their son." Such labels not only erase the person who existed before sorrow set in, they make it that much harder for a person to find their way through the haze of grief as they work to gain their footing in their "new," forever changed life.

On this day as I watched people's often-flailing attempts (my own included) to console my friend, I had a keen sense that while most people truly want to help in a time of sorrow, they often feel uncertain what to say or do. That's when it occurred to me that while there is a rich library of books by professionals designed to help the bereaved navigate their way through grief, there are very few books that offer guidance for the friends, relatives, and colleagues who want to lend useful support. Especially a book by people who actually experienced the loss. How helpful it would be, I thought, to have a book that offers specific suggestions for what to say and do—and, just as important, what not to say or do.

But where to find such advice? And how to gather a wide array of suggestions? Loss, after all, comes in many guises (loss of a child, a spouse, a parent, a friendship, a job, one's health). Moreover, to state the maybe not-so obvious, not everyone grieves in the same way. Where one person might want to be surrounded constantly by friends, for instance, another might prefer to be left in solitude.

To get this project up and running, I turned to a colleague and writer, Jen Jones. Together, we decided that in order to gather a cross section of experiences and suggestions, we would reach out through author sites, blogs, Craigslist, and friendship networks to find our contributors. We also sought input from several celebrities who had previously gone public with their stories of grappling with health loss. In addition to asking that our contributors share some aspect of their grief experience, we asked them to answer four questions:

* Best thing someone did or said?
* Worst thing someone did or said?
* Advice for someone going through a similar experience?
* Advice for those surrounding the bereaved?

Our contributors' hard-won insights and heartfelt advice fill the pages of this book. If a suggestion or idea herein helps even one person navigate the difficult what-to-say/what-to-do terrain, which in turn helps a grieving person to cope with their grief, Jen and I will have accomplished our mission.

—Shelly Fisher

A Part of Us Died

| Lisa Liem |

Stephanie Yen-Mun Liem Azar was born on July 14, 1987, "inviting everybody to join her world," as her brother puts it. At a very young age, Stephanie decided that there was a purpose in everything she did, that something good would evolve when shit happened— that her life was worth living if she could make a difference for just one person. She accomplished all this and more in her very short life. I am so blessed that I told her many times how much I love her and that she was a child whom one could only dream of.

A high-achieving individual, Stephanie earned an organ performance diploma from the Curtis Institute of Music. She then did research at Harvard before attending Columbia College of Physicians and Surgeons. It was during her medical school rotations that she contracted pneumonia with a virus. Even Columbia medicine could not save her. Stephanie died five days after she turned twenty-six, less than four weeks after marrying the love of her life.

Now, more than two years later, my husband and I still ricochet between shock and reality. Unless you really do, please refrain from telling us you know or understand exactly how we feel and how in time we will get over it. With time, our grief is not less; it is deeper. We've learned how to make that less apparent to the many people who want us to be okay. But we are not. We lost our child. We have no way out!

We receive great comfort from family and friends who have done so much to honor Stephanie and to keep her memory alive. We appreciate those who are there for us, just listening when we go crazy with grief. Part of us died with the passing of our child, and there is nothing anybody can do to make us whole again. I ask for compassion and tolerance free of comparison, judgment, or advice.

In memory of Stephanie (1987-2013)

Best thing someone did or said:
When people listen and take the initiative to do things that keep her memory alive.

Worst thing someone did or said:
Tell us they "know" or "understand," though they have never lost a child.

Advice for someone going through a similar experience:
Try not to be frustrated with people who say you will "get over it." It's usually their inept way of expressing hope that you will be okay.

Advice for those surrounding the bereaved:
Be patient. Don't offer comparisons, judgment, or advice. Just be there and listen.

New Loss

Excuses, Excuses

| Johnny Crowder |

I know you said you didn't want me stopping by every day and that I needed to move on, but I had to come visit today because I wrote you another letter and bought you some new flowers and I didn't want them to sit at my house and, besides, I missed you.

Tomorrow I probably won't have time anyway, which is good because I need to take a break like you said and besides I have a ton of work to do and I've been spending so much on gas just to get out there every day, so hopefully tomorrow will be day one of "moving on."

That isn't to say that I don't want to see you tomorrow because I do, I really do, but I'm trying to do what you said, because I know you wouldn't want me living like this, but it's just that it's so hard to go a whole day without seeing you, but I have to get used to it I guess, because I can't spend my whole life standing at your headstone wishing I was sleeping next to you.

Best thing someone did or said:
Someone told me that death is a relief, a release of pain. It calmed me to think that a passing soul experiences peace following death.

Worst thing someone did or said:
Someone offered only these words: "Life goes on." It was so insensitive. Tough love doesn't work in situations like this.

Advice for someone going through a similar experience:
* The lines of communication with a loved one are never closed off or blocked.
* The loss of a physical body does not constitute the loss of a soul.
* You can always talk to your friends and family. Reach out and you will be heard.

Advice for those surrounding the bereaved:
* Help them understand that love is eternal. It knows no boundaries or limitations.
* Be delicate and gentle, letting them know that they are not alone during this time, and they never will be.
* When it comes to healing, a sound support system can make all the difference. Just being there for someone in their time of need is paramount.

Day One

| Nikki Cee |

The nurse switched off the machines and retreated to the corner. Mum's stoic heart kept beating on the screen above Dad's head. Twice in the last two weeks we'd heard the alarm go off. Twice that jagged line had gone flat. Twice the room had filled with pastel-wrapped angels, bustling over her with wires and tubes and needles and solemn efficiency. More than twice we'd all been pushed aside so they could be heroes and we could be helpless.

Now we could draw near and wait for the alarm. This time, they wouldn't come. This time, it would be the end for them and the beginning for us. Dad held her left hand in his and fingered her gold band. After a long stretch, all of us so transfixed by our own pain that we could offer no comfort to each other, he began to speak—just to her. The hospital, with all its smells and noises and hope, fell away and his quiet, tear-stained words crawled into the silence. " . . . to hold from this day forward, for better for worse, for richer for poorer, in sickness and in health, to love and to cherish . . ."

And when the machine could bear no more, it conceded, " . . . till death do us part."

For mum, 2011 and every day since

Best thing someone did or said:
I dreaded anyone asking me how I was. How do you answer that? The most comfortable people to be around were those who said very little, judged even less, and listened when I was ready to speak. An aunt whom I wasn't especially close to filled this role. She didn't offer advice or burden me with her grief, but her quiet strength made me feel less alone.

Worst thing someone did or said:
People say all sorts of bizarre things, but you take in what is good and try to dismiss the rest. It was my own reflection while dressing for my mother's funeral that caught me unawares. One minute, I was a little girl sitting on the end of the bed waiting for Mummy to buckle my shoes. The next minute, I was trying to apply make-up to a face that was growing into that of my mother.

Advice for someone going through a similar experience:
  * It's okay to keep talking to the person who has died. Sometimes it feels like the only sane thing *to* do.
  * We all deal with grief differently, so forgive others who may handle it differently than you.
  * It does get easier; hang in there.

Advice for those surrounding the bereaved:
*Show that you care without handing out unsolicited advice. If you need to vent, find someone who is removed from the grief.
*People can eat only so much meatloaf. Ask someone close to the grieving family what sort of meals they'd like.

Ashes to Ashes

| Jennifer Gerry |

Today my brothers, stepmother, and I submitted my father's ashes to be interred. We arrived at the cemetery reserved for military vets, dressed in the last of our mourning attire, and handed the urn to what appeared to be a maintenance worker. He climbed a small ladder, placing my father almost out of our reach, and I teared up as the door of the small niche closed. Everything happened so suddenly. Sickness. Death. Service. In no time at all, he joined his brethren in this large wall . . . Final. At least it seemed final, but then I noticed something. The plaque to inform all others of this niche was missing. In fact, many of the placards were temporary, each niche awaiting their seal. Relief. This process was not yet over.

My father's death came quickly. His exit was gracious and clean, and he left us with nothing but good memories and love. He was, however, the sun to our solar system, and it was difficult losing that. As time passes, no one is spinning out into space. There's no crashing . . . no burning. His warmth is still there and our planets continue to orbit as they did before.

This process reminded me that we are all on a nonstop trajectory. Sometimes, we are barely hanging on; other times, we pull forward to distance ourselves from the past. We ever engage in routines and rituals that mask our heartaches—a game for which there is no end—only slowly developing glimpses of new beginnings.

Dedicated to William Gerry

Best thing someone did or said:
For the analytic mind, idle time only leads to intense contemplation. The best thing someone did for me during this process was provide me with a specific task: Create a chronology of my father's life through photographs. In the collection and arrangement of these photos, I had some purpose and I grew to know him better.

Worst thing someone did or said:
It's tough to identify a worst thing someone did or said. All acts of condolence, be they aligned with your grieving process or not, come from a place of pure intention. The most difficult one for me to stomach was people's unsolicited interpretations about my relationship with my father. For instance, I was woeful that we didn't get enough opportunities to know each other or to better understand what motivated our actions. A seemingly appropriate response was to provide insight into what he *probably* thought. For me, this felt intrusive. How could anyone know the inner workings of our relationship? These comments perturbed me and stopped me from sharing further. Everyone is different, though. Condolences I found particularly difficult to swallow may provide comfort for others.

(continued on next page)

(continued from previous page)

Advice for someone going through a similar experience:
One of my brothers gave me some interesting and helpful advice: let friends, spouses, and significant others share in your experience. Even if you prefer to grieve in solitude, allow others to speak their words of empathy, condolence, and sorrow. While it may seem like a bitter pill, you may find yourself surprised and bolstered by their words and perspectives.

Advice for those surrounding the bereaved:
If you are waiting for the grieving to say that they need you, they probably won't. Make food, watch TV, and just be there to fill the idle time.

An Acute Sense of Loss

| Micky Z. |

Some of them told me:
"Be strong"

Others assured me:
"She's in a better place"

I often heard:
"At least she's not suffering anymore"

There was no shortage of:
"She wouldn't want you to be so sad"

The less patient wonder when and if I'll
"move on"

No one told me . . .
that my heart would feel so heavy

No one warned me . . .
that even the good times would feel a little empty

No one properly explained . . .
that almost anything could retrigger the sorrow

No one shared the reality . . .
that grief is forever

And my Mom, the one person
I most need to talk with about this . . .
is the person I'm mourning

In memory of Mom

Best thing someone did or said:
I was given a book about the grieving process—a workbook of sorts—that helped me to see more clearly how death is perceived within our culture.

Worst thing someone did or said:
I wouldn't say it was "the worst," but the almost robotic repetition of standard condolences grew wearying.

Advice for someone going through a similar experience:
* Don't feign strength you don't feel.
* Allow yourself to process the grief in any way that feels appropriate for you, and for as long as it takes.
* Be ready to forgive lots of well-meaning, but not very helpful comments.

Advice for those surrounding the bereaved:
* Don't assume you know what a grieving person is feeling.
* Ask how you can help.
* Be present.

Change

| Judy Chaikin |

If time is kind
The streets where we walked
Will all be turned into freeways
The stores where we shopped
Will be closed for good
The house where we lived
Will be torn down.

If time is cruel
Everything will stay
The same
And everywhere
I will be reminded
Of you.

In memory of my husband, Jules

Best thing someone did or said:
Held me, hugged me, reminded me of the good times.

Worst thing someone did or said:
"It doesn't matter what he wanted . . . he should have been buried, not cremated."

Advice for someone going through a similar experience:
Don't make any big decisions for at least a year.

Advice for those surrounding the bereaved:
Give lots of hugs. The warm human connection is what is lost.

Teal is the Color of Loss

| Jaime Herndon |

I called my dead aunt's cell phone. Her numbers are still in my contact list, and I figured I'd call and see what happened. I don't know what I was expecting, but I tapped the screen and it started to ring. A man with a Spanish accent picked up, and I actually asked if Edith Rose was there, and he said I had the wrong number. Like she never existed.

In memory of Edith Rose Dawson

Best thing someone did or said:
They simply sent texts or emails telling me they were available to talk if I needed them. I couldn't call people during the period my aunt was dying from ovarian cancer, or after her death because of the emotional energy it took. Texts and emails were best, and I appreciated them.

Worst thing someone did or said:
Distanced themselves from me.

Advice for someone going through a similar experience:
Grief is exhausting. Be kind to yourself, take care of yourself, and get lots of rest.

Advice for those surrounding the bereaved:
* Do things for them, unasked, like bring them coffee or ice cream or something they like.
* Reach out and let them know you're there.
* Don't be upset or take it personally if they don't respond.

Rolling Credits

| Laura Martin |

For the past seven months
(By the time you read this, it will be more,
surely)
I have been dictating
Narratives in my head
About this period

The story sometimes is
A two-hour piece, presented
In cinematic gild
Climaxes never being false
Or unsatisfying

But they often are, or were,
So then it becomes a saga
An epic of proportions most can't fathom
So long that many grow tired
And get up from their seats
And ask for their money back

I get no refund.

More often than not the story
If that's what it is
Is told as how it seemed when trying
To look back

Discombobulated, disjointed, displaced
Time oozing or skipping
But never moving at a pace
Easy to manage
Or explain

And then it is told
In the last narrative that is the hardest
For most listeners to grasp, so I don't
Often tell it like this

It is one day, not even
One full day, from wake ups to
Lay downs, where the images loop
Without cutting on the same day
Shot of the eyes opening
And shutting

And in between the same steps
The autopilot woman
Or girl, with a woman's face
Or woman, with a girl's fear
Going through the motions
Of that one day, over and over

The loop does not cease
Until the heart, which the tumor drains slowly,
Drains it until it no longer
Beats the way
The heart
Should
Beat.

In memory of my mother, Debra Martin

Best thing someone did or said:
Being there for me when I didn't ask.

Worst thing someone did or said:
Trying to tell me their own story of their mom or dad passing or telling me they understood how I was feeling. Or saying that they would be there in a second if I needed them, and then not showing up.

Advice for someone going through a similar experience:
You really have to rely on yourself, but do not shut out everyone around you. It will only hurt you in the long run.

Advice for those surrounding the bereaved:
Do not think that my ability to move on with my life means that it does not still pain me every day to think of her.

Making Merry without Mary

| Katherine Tomlinson |

My sister died last year, but the pain of her loss is a wound only freshly healed over. Beneath the new pink skin is tender flesh, filled with nerve endings firing at random. The ache isn't constant, but comes unexpectedly, triggered by the most innocuous things. The scent of peppermint. The taste of salty caramel. A glimpse of *Miracle on 34th Street* while clicking through to the news.

My sister loved Christmas. I loved my sister. The two feelings are now inextricably twined.

In memory of Mary Beth Tomlinson

Best thing someone did or said:
A friend gave me a gift certificate for a massage, and it was just what I needed.

Worst thing someone did or said:
I was making phone calls to the people in my sister's address book, and I got to one of her friends whom I also knew. When I told him that Mary had died, he launched into an account of some argument he'd been having with her and how it had made him feel. I'm usually a pretty patient person, but I just wanted to smack him.

Advice for someone going through a similar experience:
* While dwelling isn't productive, don't bury your feelings. Talk them out or write them down.
* Avoid the temptation to burrow into your shell and deal with your grief by yourself.
* At the same time, don't let yourself get sucked into a vortex of negative energy. You may have friends (I know I do) who can't stop poking bruises to see if they still hurt. "How *are* you?" a friend would ask, face scrunched up with concern. Even if the answer might have been, "Fine," a minute ago, I would feel my mood plummet.

(continued on next page)

(*continued from previous page*)

 * Eat more protein than usual because it will help curb the impulse to eat a lot of sugar. (I stuffed down my feelings and gained nearly thirty pounds before I snapped out of it.)
 * Be kind to yourself. It's okay to be sad.

Advice for those surrounding the bereaved:
 * Do not say, "Sorry for your loss." That's the default expression of sympathy that all the cops and EMTs use. While I believe it's sincere, if perfunctory, I remember thinking, as I heard it for the billionth time, "I will never, ever, ever say this."
 * Offer practical help. Sorrow can be paralyzing, and there are always things that need to be done. But don't say, "Is there something I can do?" A vague offer like that is likely to meet with, "No, I'm fine." Instead, be specific. "Do you need a ride to the funeral home?" "Do you want me to take stuff to Goodwill?" "Can I help you clean out his apartment?" Offer options.
 * A grieving person is going through so many emotions. Let them talk.

The Littlest Things

| Rohini Venkatraman |

Now that my grandma's gone, it's the little things I remember most vividly. Nine years ago, for instance, I remember standing outside my college bookstore, staring at my phone. My grandma had just undergone surgery to remove a cancerous lump in her breast. I wanted to call her, but didn't know what to say. After practicing various conversations in my head, I finally dialed the number.

"Hello?"

When I heard her voice, the best I could manage was, "Hi, it's me. Are you okay?"

My grandma chuckled. "I'm fine. How are you?" We then had a conversation just like any other. She asked about the goings-on in my life. I filled her in on the details. She always did that, my grandma. Put others before herself. She wasn't one to dwell on her surgery. She was too strong a woman for that.

Another time I visited her in Chennai. I was feeling a bit awkward because I hadn't visited her for several years. The second I walked through the door, she looked me up and down. One of those maternal assessments. "Your nose looks great," she said casually, as if we'd seen each other just yesterday. "I was really worried about your nose when you were younger. It looked kind of pressed in. It looks much better now." The really little things.

My grandma's cancer returned three years ago and spread quickly. When she passed away in her sleep, she looked quite peaceful, I'm told. That she is no longer suffering, that she is now reunited with her husband, my late grandpa, makes me tearfully content.

But on the day she died and I was in a fog, it was little things that pushed through to grab my attention. A smile on a friend's face. The crisp autumn air. Looking back, that seems a fitting tribute. My grandma was an appreciator of the small things. She gave that to me.

Here's to the little things.

In memory of my grandma,
Kantha Chandramouli (1935–2011)

Best thing someone did or said:
I feel that death is always accompanied by regret-filled sadness—this little piece of you that wishes you had talked just one more time, been together just one more time. The best advice I received during the grieving period was to remember the wonderful conversations we did get to have and the experiences we did get to share together, rather than what we didn't.

Worst thing someone did or said:
I surrounded myself with loved ones during this period, all of who understood what I was going through (some of who, family members, were going through it as well). Because of this, I wouldn't necessarily say that there were any "bad" things that someone said or did.

Advice for someone going through a similar experience:
Remember the good times that you had together. Resist the urge to dwell on what could have been different or what you wish you had said or done. Think about the littlest moments. Those will make the biggest difference in uplifting your spirit.

Advice for those surrounding the bereaved:
Gauge from the individual how they want to deal with the situation. Some people like to talk about things. Others like to be surrounded by people in silence. Others like to be alone. Not everyone is the same. The best thing you can do is understand how a particular individual wants to be treated.

Sudden Loss

Losing Stephen

| Mar Christi |

The call came out of the blue, like that lightning they talk about striking on a sunny day.

You answer, "Hello," and know by the tone of the caller's voice your world has changed.

Then the brief time when you wait for someone to call back, to say there was a mistake, that Stephen really isn't dead after all. But that call never comes.

The loss of one's mother or dad . . . of an elderly aunt or uncle . . . these events have their own sadness. Yet they are comprehensible; they follow an ancient order.

But to hear of the passing of your twenty-six-year-old nephew . . . There are no words.

And there were no words I knew to say to my brother . . . to hear the agony in his voice telling me of the passing of his son.

When the older generation passes, you know you've lost a piece of your past. The world you knew, grew up in, is gone. Times that won't be again. When my mother passed away and I felt weird, my cousin Richard told me that losing your parents was like losing the pillars that held up your world. That now things will change. That I will feel differently as I stand alone.

But to lose a nephew . . . you lose the future. And you realize that this future, though unformed, held plans, ideas, and hopes that you weren't even aware of as you went about the business of living.

I'm grateful to the cousins who called my brother to speak with him. Though they thought their efforts inadequate, I know their expressions of comfort helped. When I spoke to my brother at the end of that endless day, he sounded more normal, more himself. The reaching out, the simple expressions that they cared, that he didn't stand alone in his grief, helped.

When a young person dies, people want to know why did this happen, what caused this tragedy, how could this occur? Their curiosity, at times, overrides their manners. Car accident? Medical crisis? I know they are only asking out of fear that somehow the event will cause echoes in their own family. They don't know how their questions sound to the grieving.

In truth, the "why," the "what," the "how" don't matter.

The only thing that matters is that Stephen is gone.

In memory of Stephen Ceres

Best thing someone did or said:
My cousins Diane and Richard were on vacation in Germany when word came about Stephen. They lit a candle for him at the Cologne Cathedral and called Stephen's father. It meant a lot to have them think of Stephen during that time. It was nice to think that Stephen had tributes on two continents.

Worst thing someone did or said:
The repetitive demand to know, "What happened?"

Advice for someone going through a similar experience:
The shock of unexpected loss literally "takes your breath away." Breathe and move your thoughts away from the sadness. One minute, one hour, one day at a time.

Advice for those surrounding the bereaved:
Grief, like happiness, is personal. Even the person who is grieving may be surprised how they experience it. So pay close attention and allow your heart, rather than your head, to guide.

A Marital Quilt

| P. C. Moorehead |

As the cards, letters, and notes piled up following Tom's death, I just collected them all and eventually placed them in large manila envelopes. I knew that at some point I would need a meaningful closure to this outpouring of kindness. When the time felt right, I decided to arrange the materials into a marital quilt. For me, a quilt symbolized the manner in which Tom's and my separate lives had been stitched together into one by relationships and love.

*In memory of my late husband,
Thomas Moorehead (1934-1991)*

Best thing someone did or said:
* For my graduate program in transpersonal psychology, I wrote several papers in which I related and discussed my grieving process. It was helpful to receive the support and comments of my professors and fellow students.
* Not long after Tom's death, our church held its annual service of remembrance to commemorate members of the congregation who had died during the previous year. The calling out of each person's name, accompanied by pictures, lit candles, and hymns, was deeply comforting.
* A neighbor brought over a pot of homemade soup. Her kindness and the warmth of the soup nourished me.
* Another neighbor shared the many humorous comments she remembered Tom making about different events. Our laughter as we recalled his remarks lightened my spirit.
* A third neighbor told me of my good fortune in experiencing such a good relationship. She reminded me that some people look for that all their lives. This helped me keep perspective about my loss.

Worst thing someone did or said:
I do not recall any such remarks or actions.

(continued on next page)

(continued from previous page)

Advice for someone going through a similar experience:
* Give yourself time to grieve and be kind to yourself.
* If a long illness was involved, forgive yourself for any caregiving lapses that may have occurred, even given your best efforts.
* Be grateful for the time you had together.

Advice for those surrounding the bereaved:
* Cut the bereaved person some slack. Grieving takes time and endurance, and the person may not always have energy or enthusiasm.
* If the grieving person seems distracted or a little shaky, offer to run errands or do the driving for that person.
* Listen, even to the silences, of the grieving person.

Here I am, Girl in Your Aftermath

| Alicen Grey |

Here I am, Girl in your aftermath
who can't look at trains
when they pull into the station.
I live in New York City.
I have to take the train twice a day.
It's been 365 days since you jumped in front of one.
You do the math.
Here I am, Girl who can't stop writing about you
though there's nothing new to say, really.
This is evidenced by the fact that
I wrote 10 drafts of this poem
and deleted all of them.
11 now.
Here I am, Girl in your aftermath,
with that money
still set aside in my bank account

to buy your train ticket here
—you know, the train ticket I said
I'd buy for you
if you managed to hang on another month.
There's probably something ironic about that
whole train thing,
but whatever,
I'm too tired to figure it out.
There goes the twelfth draft.
Why do I even
bother.
There you were, Boy,
storm-starter,
mess-maker,
ticking death bomb that left
grief-shrapnel
as far as the heart can see;
there you were, the
love of my life and
the pain I will carry until my own end comes;
there you were, tiptoeing on the Amtrak platform,
looking down the track,
watching the train intensely as it came into the station,
watching the train the way I can't watch the train
anymore
thanks to you;
there you were,
thinking no one
would notice you
gone.
How dare you
think

such a thing.
I'm starting to understand what they mean
when they say it's normal to be angry
at people who commit suicide.
Sometimes I might even
hate you.
Here I am, Girl in your aftermath
on the thirteenth draft of a poem
that says pretty much the same thing
that the first, second, third, fourth, fifth, sixth, seventh,
eighth, ninth, tenth, eleventh, and twelfth
drafts did,
and just like all the other drafts,
this one doesn't have an ending,
no,
this one goes on
kind of awkwardly
kind of desperately
and very painfully,
like the way you made us do
after you.

To Roman, my lion
(August 1, 1987—September 24, 2014)

Best thing someone did or said:
My wonderful partner, Mickey, invited me over as soon as I told him the news and let me grieve for an entire day: crying non-stop, playing sad music, reminiscing about my favorite memories of Roman . . . anything that helped.

Worst thing someone did or said:
"I'm so glad *my* friends aren't suicidal!"

Advice for someone going through a similar experience:
Continue talking to your deceased loved one. Tell them how you feel. Tell them about your day. Whenever you miss them, ask them to send you a sign.

Advice for those looking to provide support to someone in a similar situation:
Don't just *say,* "I'm here for you." Actually be there.

Balloons of Love

| Valerie Benko |

The muddy gravel driveway crunched beneath my tires as I pulled up to the one-story ranch house set on a cement slab. The lawn was lush and vibrant from the spring rains. A cluster of purple flowers poked through the earth by the front porch. I was really going to miss this place.

In the warm sunshine, I joined family members gathered on the front lawn. Hushed voices filled the air as balloons were handed to each guest. I tugged on the string of the blue Mylar balloon I was holding so the star shape hid my tear-stained face. My other hand clutched a black permanent marker. I was supposed to write a message on the balloon to my paternal grandmother, who had just unexpectedly joined my grandfather in the afterlife. But I didn't know what to say.

I wish I could say my grandmother was the stereotypical fuzzy, warm, loving type who spoiled me with trinkets and fresh baked goodies, but she wasn't. She was strongly opinionated, given to saying exactly what was on her mind. She praised us only if we did something extraordinary.

For all that my grandmother wasn't, there was a lot that she was. As I peeked from behind my shiny balloon at the rest of my family, I wondered what was going to happen to us cousins, uncles, and siblings. My grandmother was the thin thread that held this part of our family together.

As everyone scribbled on their balloons, I stared at the blank surface of mine. What to write? I tried to remember the last thing Gram said to me that was meaningful. Then it came to me, "You're the one to watch." I'll never forget that toothless grin as she bent toward me to show the piece of paper clutched in her hand. It was a children's story I had published recently online, my very first accepted piece as a freelance writer and not as a journalist. Now that my moment of praise had arrived, Gram's pride felt paramount. It didn't matter if I ever became a big name in the publishing world; I was already a star in her eyes.

The memory brought fresh tears, but I now knew what I wanted to say. I wrote, "You loved, you laughed, you cried. You may be gone, but my words will keep you alive." Then, I held the balloon close to my heart.

As the chorus of "Angels Among Us" boomed from car speakers, everyone released their balloons. Red, blue, gold, pink, white, and green balloons carrying messages of love and closure floated above the tree tops then lifted high into the sky—except mine. Tangled with extra, unused balloons that bore no message, it drifted down the street about five feet off the ground.

I was aghast! If a car came around the bend, it would collide with this tangled mess and my message would never get to heaven. Suddenly, there was a shift in the wind and a current of air, like a tiny prayer, lifted the flotilla. As it cleared the treetops, cheers rang out.

The balloons rose higher and higher, soon a bright speck against the white clouds. I smiled as the last balloon disappeared from sight. I knew Gram wouldn't let my message get away.

Dedicated to my grandmother,
Mary Jean Hoffmann (1929-2010)

Best thing someone did or said:
The best thing someone did for me was to sit with me in silence and let me cry. Just knowing that person was there for me and that I was not alone was enough.

Worst thing someone did or said:
Colleagues had good intentions by approaching me about my grandmother's passing and wanting me to talk about it, but I just wanted to be left alone so I wouldn't start crying at work.

Advice for someone going through a similar experience:
* Forgetting the pain doesn't mean forgetting the person.
* Grieving takes time and it's different for everyone.
* It's okay if people see you cry. You're human.

Advice for those surrounding the bereaved:
* Offer support that reflects your usual level of interaction with the grieving individual. If you barely interact with them at work, for example, express your condolences and move on.
* Only offer time and services if you mean it.
* When preparing food dishes for the grieving family, keep children in mind and make something special for them.

Moments to Savor

| Kathy Larson |

We have traveled down whimsical paths
that led us hither and yon and back again,
all while never leaving the office.
We talked about the joys of sons and daughters,
the vagaries of spouses, challenges of work,
the pain of teenagers, neediness of old age.
Spoke of the anguish that comes with illness,
the pleadings for miracles for our loved ones.

If I had known that one day a message would
arrive, unexpectedly—He has suffered and gone.
He is at peace.—I would not have been so careless with
your words.
I would have savored them, to pore over and glean
small comfort when the night closes in
and I feel bereft and lonely.

In memory of my colleague, David

Best thing someone did or said:
The best thing my family and friends did was to let me express my thoughts uninterrupted and not try to fix my grief. A supportive shoulder to lean on helped me the most.

Worst thing someone did or said:
The worst thing someone said was, "This will pass." There is no timetable for grief. No one can say how long your pain will last. Each of us grieves in a different manner.

Advice for someone going through a similar experience:
* Let yourself grieve. Do not hold it in.
* Allow yourself, without guilt, to disengage from normal for a time.
* Lean on those who offer support and allow them to help you.

Advice for those surrounding the bereaved:
* Words are not necessary.
* Food is important.
* Loving smiles help.

10 Things I Would Tell You if You Were Still Here

| Jami Kahn |

i. i always hated that *Simpsons* shirt you used to wear.

ii. i'm sorry that i didn't tell you i loved you before you walked out the door that night. i tell you nearly every hour now, and it doesn't make an ounce of difference.

iii. i think i kissed a ghost last night, but i'm not sure if it was you.

iv. i'll make you a deal: come back, and you can have as much of the bed as you want. hogging the blanket is only fun if there's someone there to steal it from.

v. i want to tell you that i hate seeing you in the faces of strangers on the street, but i would be lying.

vi. people keep asking me how i'm doing, like you were a sprained ankle or a broken nail. i tell them i have phantom limb syndrome, and they just frown, like i'm hopeless. (maybe they're right.)

vii. i know that there is an "acceptable" time for mourning, but i don't think i will be able to turn this off when that time comes.

viii. i talk to you every day. it would be nice to hear back every once in a while.

ix. somehow it's my fault. they say it's just survivor's guilt, but they're wrong. there is no fathomable explanation for why i am here and you are not.

x. i don't know what i'll do when i stop feeling your presence in absolutely everything.

Best thing someone did or said:
"I'm sorry for you."

Worst thing someone did or said:
"They're in a better place, now."

Advice for someone going through a similar experience:
* Put offers of help to good use.
* Make your needs clear.

Advice for those surrounding the bereaved:
* Be a good listener.
* Don't project your assumptions and opinions onto the grieving individual; everybody grieves differently.

Message to a Friend

| Deanna Young |

I lost a friend today. Those five words aren't poignant, by any means. I've lost count of all those I have lost over the years, my father included. This isn't exactly my first rodeo.

I do not write these words for me. No, this has nothing to do with how I feel because one less boy walks this earth today, an absence of his own making, his own choice. This isn't like other missed opportunities for good-byes. This time, something very different, very real occurred to me: Suicide isn't reserved exclusively for selfish monsters or bad people, even.

I don't feel compelled to illustrate or convince, because it will do my friend no justice. He wasn't just some boy who walked this earth aimlessly, searching for a purpose he failed to find. I wish I knew what it was that he *was* searching for. I do know that his was a heart filled solely with pure intent. To take your own life, to admit that this life has consumed you to the point where to go on would be too painful, suggests a longing for a clean slate this life could never offer.

He made the choice to end a pain we choose not to understand because we don't consider it normal. I don't berate myself.

Hide and seek is an impossible game to play when a person hides with the intention of never again being found. But that doesn't mean we should ever stop looking. People rarely ask for the things they need.

These words are a sad, human attempt to grapple with death. I do not want to say good-bye, because that suggests we will never meet again, and I'm far too optimistic to accept that. Instead, I want to say only, *I understand, and you are loved.*

In memory of a friend, Ian Mautner (1994-2014)

Best thing someone did or said:
"You are loved."

Worst thing someone did or said:
"Everything happens for a reason."

Advice for someone going through a similar situation:
* Speak up at times when no one else will.
* Be kind to everyone you encounter and listen when others need to talk.
* Don't wait for something tragic to affect your life before you realize the importance of empathy and friendship.

Advice for those surrounding the bereaved:
* Avoid making statements of certainty when giving advice for coping. Instead, try to listen, understand, and offer advice with the acknowledgment that not all people will share your perspective on a situation.
* Try to understand that, as individuals, we all experience tragedy and triumph in wildly different manners.

No Sad Farewell

| S. Conroy |

I don't know if you knew
that I knew you were there
that last time you sat
so quietly in a chair
between the fridge
and the kitchen table.

No brandishing of the "rat's tail,"
no stories of raucous import,
no "pull my finger," "taxi!"
or any such toilet-sport.

And thus I affected
with such assiduous care
not to notice your company
or revel in your being there,
knowing full well
if I were to look at you full on
that there would be no sad farewell
you would just be gone,
leaving me in the kitchen
alone in my dream.

In memory of my brother, Maxim

Best thing someone did or said:

My brother was thirty-two years old when he died suddenly and quite horrifically. Here one day, gone the next. Fortunately, I have a lot of siblings who were in the same situation, and my best friend had known my brother from childhood. So while we were all pretty zombified, shocked, at the funeral, at least we understood each other. But I live abroad, and when I returned home after the funeral, I was surrounded by people who did not know him. The best thing friends did during this time was to listen when I needed to talk about my brother—and at the time I did need to talk quite a lot. It kept him alive a little longer (although in the beginning, I couldn't use the past tense; it felt too brutal). I don't think I've ever thanked these friends for being there and listening to me ramble on about someone they never knew.

Worst thing someone did or said:

* Around the time of the funeral, I kept hearing this well-meaning phrase, "Time will heal." It felt almost obscene, disrespectful of my brother. I feel very ungrateful even mentioning that this phrase was not comforting. People were just being kind, and retrospectively I can appreciate their kindness. But at the time it felt clichéd.

* One of my language students, practicing his English, asked, "How many brothers and sisters have you got?" It

(continued on next page)

(continued from previous page)

came out of the blue. I just wasn't prepared. Such a simple question and I had to leave the room.

* When I told a close friend how my brother had died, he said he was sorry, but he couldn't hear it. I think I had transferred the bleakness within me, and it was too much for him. At the time, it made me feel like a freak who could only drag others down with my sadness.

Advice for someone going through a similar experience:

* Talk about your loved one and how you are feeling, don't bottle it up. Get bereavement therapy, if you need it, or at least find a place where you can scream if you need to.
* Spend as much time as possible with people you love and who knew the deceased person.
* I don't know if it would work for others, but writing letters to my deceased brother helped and kept him alive in some abstract way. I was very honest in these letters, much more honest than I had ever been to his face. Sometimes I rambled on about the weather, told him what was happening in the world; sometimes I told him how I envied him this or that, was sorry for A, thought he should apologize for B, but I'd forgive him now that he was dead (!) etc., etc. . . .

Advice for those surrounding the bereaved:

* Listen to them, but don't force them to talk.
* Be patient with their moods. And if they withdraw, don't take it personally. Sometimes in that bereaved state, trying to act normal in social situations is extremely draining.
* Let them cry. It's natural.

In Search of Peace

| Setareh Makinejad |

A month after the unexpected passing of my dear daughter, Shahdi, friends and relatives started encouraging me to stop wearing black. My polite response was that I would abandon the color of mourning when I reached some level of peace with this colossal tragedy that had transformed my life into an abyss of regrets, longing, and sorrow.

Five months later, I am still wearing black. It fits my mood, which is still shrouded under dense black clouds that belong to the savage storm that invaded my life after Shahdi's death and is only slightly letting up lately. On the virtual island where I now reside, the island of "Unfortunate Parents," it rains without pause. If I reach some level of peace, I might be able to move into a neighborhood on this island where the lightning and winds are less intense, the rain intermittent.

To reach even that level of peace, I have to travel long and far, as many ill-fated parents before me have traveled, among them my own grandmothers. I believe the only path to reach peace after losing a child is to relearn how to live, this time without one's child, this time without part of one's own heart and soul.

When I was thirty-one years old, my beloved Shahdi joined me on my life journey, eager to have her first Mommy-made nourishment. My other travel companions were Mehrdad and Arman. Shahdi brought so much joy, happiness, intelligence, beauty, and talent to our ensemble for almost twenty years. With her gone, we lost one of the four pillars of our life journey. Now, I have to learn how to make the rest of my journey tolerable without her at my side.

Contrary to popular belief, the milestones (birthdays, holidays, etc.) are not the most difficult challenge. Rather, it's the everyday events. The first time I entered a grocery store, two weeks after Shahdi's passing, I became so overwhelmed with sorrow and despair that I had to leave the store. These last five months, I have encountered such moments countless times. In shops. Parks. Malls. Neighborhoods. Restaurants. Around our house. In our backyard.

I suppose the best way to describe the sorrow and longing is to think of one's heart as if it were made of thousands of little glass jars, with each jar holding a precious memory. As I have been going through the grieving process, I have lost many of these glass jars. They usually break when I find myself in an experience where I am consumed by sorrow. Like when I opened the kitchen cupboard and found Shahdi's half-finished box of hot chocolate there. Or when I bought raspberries and strawberries, but Shahdi wasn't there to enjoy them so they sat idle in the refrigerator for days. Or when I washed her bedding and put it away. Forever.

As time goes by, fewer jars will remain to be broken. At some point, if I ever reach peace, my heart will have only a limited number of jars left. These jars are the strong ones that will never break, because the memories they contain will have gone through the grieving process so many times that they will no longer leave me feeling brokenhearted.

One is expected gradually to become desensitized to the point where one can recall the memories without breaking down or suffering a wrench of sorrow. I hope someday to reach that point.

*In Memory of My Light, My Joy, My Love,
My Daughter, Shahdi M. Negahban
(December 22, 1993–November 26, 2013)*

Best thing someone did or said:

* Someone told me that I should take my time to grieve my beautiful daughter, Shahdi, and that is exactly how I have approached this colossal tragedy. I do not expect my grieving to end while I am alive. Therefore, I have come to terms with the fact that I will break down from time to time for the rest of my life, sometimes in the most awkward places and at the most inopportune times. That is okay with me. Shahdi deserves a lot more than occasional melancholy periods through the rest of my life. Shahdi is a part of me and will be with me for as long as I live.

* The best therapy for me during the last nine months has been Shahdi's memorial page on Facebook, which was created by the mother of Shahdi's best friend. Sharing my thoughts on Shahdi and our grief has been tremendously comforting to me. Writing about Shahdi has given me the means to keep her memory alive. To know that she is not yet forgotten gives me great comfort.

Worst thing someone did or said:
A cruel person sent me a text a month ago saying that had I been a good mother, my daughter would not have taken her own life.

Advice for someone going through a similar situation:
Each person dealing with grief has to find his/her own path to peace. There is no one formula. Grieving is a very personal

and lonely process, and one must be prepared for an emotional roller coaster. One should not hasten the grief process to please others, but rather must take their time to fully experience all the raw and painful emotions. Gradually, one gets to the longing and sorrow, and finally accepts the finality of the loss. However, one will never be the same as before and life's priorities certainly change. The loss of my daughter made me accept death as my friend, because I know someday it will lead me to my beloved Shahdi. Thus, I am no longer afraid of death. This change by itself has been very liberating.

Advice for those surrounding the bereaved:

* Please do not tell grieving parents that their deceased child is now in a better place. Nobody knows that for sure. If one is not religious, such a statement is very hollow and silly.

* The best thing is to acknowledge the enormity of their loss and pain. Give them the freedom to grieve for their child in their own way. Give them as much time as they need. Don't tell them how frequently to cry or how often they should visit the cemetery. Even if you are a bereaved parent, recognize that individuals are different; a person's approach to grief could be different than yours.

* Give the bereaved parents love and support. Don't leave them alone, or they may immerse themselves in old memories and fall into depression.

After Your Fatal Jump

| Eve West Bessier |

In the soft pumping
chambers of the heart,
an element of sorrow
can harden to resentment,
creating abrasive sediment.

Unlike the oyster,
wherein grit stimulates
layers of lustrous white
in the fertile dark,
creating a pearl;

the heart that closes
on inconsolable loss
secretes no miraculous gloss
to coat the irritant
for radiant gain.

The heart can only create
its luminosity
by hurling clear
the calculus
of the unresolved,

exposing pain
to the ocean salt
of self-transparency.

In memory of my ex-husband, Gregory (1959-2012)

Best thing someone did or said:
Allow the feelings to move through like a powerful thunderstorm. Don't deny the feelings or try to hold them back. After the flash flood, there will be peace. Healing is not about "fixing" anything. Healing is about accepting what is.

Worst thing someone did or said:
"Just get over it, and move on."

Advice for someone going through a similar experience:
* Treat yourself with the utmost kindness and gentleness, as you would a small child.
* Feel absolutely everything you are feeling, but give yourself enough space to not act on any of those feelings while they are raging, especially the raw and angry ones. Feeling your anger is healing, but acting out of your anger can become harmful.

Advice for those looking to provide support to someone in a similar situation:
* Listen; allow the person to experience being heard.
* Resist trying to "fix" anything, or trying to "cheer" them up.
* Tell them you respect their courage in truly grieving the loss.

V

| Melanie Bell |

You stopped us in front of the cathedral,
Windows tangerine and copper, translucent in the dark,
And said "Spontaneous," your word
Doled out every day like pennies at the corner store,
"Let's give spontaneous thanks for the beautiful things."
We stood there in front of glassy saints,
Five college kids,
And did.

You lived by theme songs—
Belting "Colors of the Wind" through an
autumn-painted campus
To annoy us until we joined in,
"Lemon Tree" in 4:00 a.m. wood-paneled rooms
Flickering with disco lights,
Limbs like starfish, bodies spiraling.
You lived alphabetically—
Valentine's birthday, Vierka (your nickname for people
that mattered), viola,
Dead at 28 in Vienna.

You took everything for free—
Ribboned skirts and corduroy clothing-swap jackets
Carried home in a Santa Claus sack,
Vegan soup kitchen dinners (your hands in suds to pay).
I thought it fearless
When you left early—never could stay
In one place long.
I didn't expect to see you again.

In Montreal we met in calf-deep snow,
In Fredericton biking a play from school to school.
Soon it was continents you pedaled over.
"To hell with reality!
I want to die in music, not in reason or in prose."
I thumb the book of quotes you wrote me
Before crossing the seven seas, simple as drinking water.

I would have e-mailed again sometime
To check: "How are you?"
Meaning "Are you still here?"
Expecting you to be.

If you could write back
I'd send you a second surprise party.
Collect old friends with potluck dishes,
Pizza, cream cake, red balloons
In that echoing wood-paneled room,
To sit and watch you laugh.

Dedicated to Viera Linderova

Best thing someone did or said:
Allowing grief and simply listening.

Worst thing someone did or said:
Platitudes, like, "Everything happens for a reason."

Advice for someone going through a similar experience:
* Allow yourself to feel the full extent of your feelings.
* Maintain structure in your life—it will keep you going.

Advice for those surrounding the bereaved:
* Listen with compassion.
* Don't offer unsolicited opinions or judge in any way.
* Don't try to sugarcoat the reality of the person's loss.

Loss With Time
for a Goodbye

A Love Filled With Laughter

| Esther M. Bailey |

Throughout our forty-one-year marriage, my husband Ray charmed me and others with his quick, dry wit. He didn't try to be funny; he just was. Like the time we were riding in the car and a song came on the radio. "What's the name of that song?" he asked.

"'Where Are the Clowns?'" I said.

"Oh," he mused. "I didn't know they were looking for me."

Even during his declining years, Ray loved to make me laugh. One day when the thought of preparing a dinner weighed heavy and I needed a menu suggestion, something beyond Ray's usual, "Whatever you want" or "Whichever is easier," I prodded him. "Would you prefer chicken pot pie or chicken-noodle casserole?" I asked. "And don't say, 'Whatever you want.'"

"Which is easier?" he said.

"They're both the same."

"Then I'll have half of each," he responded.

I doubt if many husbands pick out the dress their wives wear to their funeral. Ray did. While we were shopping for Christmas one year, he noticed a striking black dress in the window of a boutique. "You don't have any black," he said. "What are you going to wear to my funeral?" He bought me the dress. Years later, I wore it to his funeral.

About six months before his death, my husband told me, his tone uncharacteristically earnest, "After I'm gone, you may meet someone you like and want to get married again. If you do, I want you to know that it's all right with me."

"I won't want to marry anyone else," I assured him.

Apparently he continued to mull the matter because a few months later, he said, "Uh, I've decided I *don't* want you to get married again."

"Okay, Sweetheart," I said, with a laugh, joy filling my heart. Oh, how this man loved me.

There was little room for laughter after Ray was transferred to a hospice facility. I had only six days to put the finishing touches on our years together. His blue eyes stayed fixed on mine as I sang "Let Me Call You Sweetheart." I told him how I'd treasured being his wife. "And you," I said, "have been a wonderful husband." His voice barely audible, he said, "Thank you for telling me that." I reminded him how, as persons of faith, we had talked often about heaven. "You will soon see your mother and your brother," I said. "And you can ask God all those questions you've wondered about."

Early the next morning the dreaded call came.

Even in my sadness, I "do not grieve as others do who have no hope" (1 Thessalonians 4:13). One day I, too, will pass from this life to a better place. I can't wait to hear how Ray will greet me. For sure, his words will give me a smile.

Best thing someone did or said:
People reminded me of good times with my husband, particularly those that highlighted Ray's sense of humor.

Worst thing someone did or said:
No one did anything bad, but the worst thing anyone could have done was to say my loss was God's will.

Advice for someone going through a similar experience:
 * Keep the person you've lost alive in your mind and heart.
 * Celebrate special events: anniversaries, birthdays, Christmas.

Advice for those surrounding the bereaved:
 * Offer lots of hugs, but few words.
 * Listen twice, but speak once.
 * Don't minimize the loss.

Last Moments

| Megan Steusloff |

I am haunted by images of those last moments. The papers had been signed and the machines turned off. What had been estimated would take minutes had stretched into hours of labored breathing. The reality was that the hospital needed the room for the next critical care patient. So, the dying man was transferred to a room on the fifth floor, a tiny, neglected room with stagnant air and dust on the small table. There were no paintings or color on the walls. It was difficult for my parents, my grandmother, and me to squeeze around the bed, and there were only two chairs. This is where the greatest man in my universe was going to take his last breath.

I remember trying to lie across the vent near the darkened window, exhausted and scared. It is a strange endeavor to sit and watch, waiting for someone you love with all your heart to succumb to inevitable death.

We all seemed to realize the obvious at the same time. We were not waiting for him. Instead, he was waiting for us. He needed us to leave. The last generous, gentle, amazing act of this man was to not allow his granddaughter see him die.

In the fourteen days he had been slipping away from us

at the hospital, the doctors had made it clear that he was not responding to anything. No poking or medication was having an effect. Yet I knew better. He knew we were there. He heard our whispered prayers and felt the tears falling from our cheeks onto his arms and hands as we clung to them. He had been letting go of us slowly, holding onto us tenderly, showing us in his own quiet way the depth of his love.

I walked deliberately over to the bed and took it all in. He looked little, thin under his blue and white checkered hospital gown. The always tan and glowing skin was gaunt and pale. The breathing was inconsistent and painful to hear. I felt selfish for wanting him to fight longer and harder, for wanting him to stay and be here for me. In that last moment we shared, I laid my head on his chest, feeling his heart against my cheek, and gently wrapped my arms up around his neck. "Thank you for everything," I said. "I love you, Grandpa." There was so much to say, to explain, to make sure he knew and understood before he went, but that was all I could manage. Thanks and love was the essence of all I felt anyway.

At the doorway, I looked back to stare at him and try to soak up the spirit of this man one last time. I felt a surge of pride that I was there for him. That I was one of the final voices he heard. That my abundant love was one of the last things he felt. That I took this opportunity to say good-bye, no matter how brave it forced me to be.

Dedicated to Paul B. Merlo, Sr.

Best thing someone did or said:
At a funeral home, I was told how much heaven had improved, how the angels must be singing, how a party was going on because my loved one had joined the ranks. It helped to think that the joy I was once given was now being shared with and felt by others. I loved the idea of his spirit and energy moving to a new place and time, but still being true to all that made him the amazing person he was.

Worst thing someone did or said:
I was once asked accusingly why I was not crying. Mourning is such a strange state to live in. Sometimes I felt sad, sometimes I laughed, sometimes I could not stop eating, sometimes I felt exhausted, and sometimes I could not contain my energy. I was a hodgepodge of emotions! To be judged for my reaction was hurtful. I had to be true to myself and cry when I needed to cry, not when others expected me to.

Advice for someone going through a similar experience:
Try to find a healthy balance between holding onto the person you've lost and moving forward with your life. Remember with all your heart and continue on with all your strength.

Advice for those surrounding the bereaved:
Try not to understand or fix them, just be there for them. Small gestures of kindness can go a long way, and offering to help with the details of life—laundry, grocery shopping, lawn mowing—can be so very thoughtful. Give space and time and encouragement. Smile and squeeze their hands. Remind them that there is still good, still hope, still love in this world to live for.

Ode to a Dearest Uncle

| J.C. Elkin |

I treasured you for 50 years
of yellowing memories

like your store of antique books
or Mom's old photographs

glossy, scalloped black and whites—
sweet lad, soldier, groom;

in postcards we bought on our trips
and ones you saved for me;

in the smell of your Old Spice cologne
and fruity pipe tobacco

fruitier than Auntie's pies
you brought us each Thanksgiving;

with cool suede hugs and warm guffaws,
humming, as I do;

in Vaudeville hits we crooned as one
in vinyl played through the groove.

You, who tagged a *Y* on my name,
and I let you. You alone.

Dedicated to Norman Loiselle (1927-1914)

Best thing someone did or said:
During that time, my husband reminded me often how much my
uncle enjoyed our times together, and that was a sweet comfort.

Worst thing someone did or said:
I am grateful that no one did or said anything inconsiderate
during that time. Perhaps our geographic distance and the fact
that he was not an immediate family member shielded me from
the kind of thoughtless comments people sometimes make
when they feel compelled to say something, to say anything,
even if they don't know what to say.

Advice for someone going through a similar experience:
   * Put into words the trait that you most admired about this
     person and make a conscious effort to emulate that.
   * Look at pictures and relive the good times.
   ** Share your thoughts with someone.

Advice for those surrounding the bereaved:
   * Let them speak without interruption or judgment (good
     or bad).
   * If the person seems receptive, a silent touch or a hug is a
     powerful balm.

The Day Before You Died

| Emily Bright |

nothing remarkable happened. Dawn
hummed with lobster boats.
Your flowers bloomed red and gold,
the same as yesterday.
Someone thought to see about lunch
and everyone took naps as usual, books
on sleeping chests rising and
sinking with the tide.

Dedicated to Lana, my grandmother (1919–2006)

Best thing someone did or said:

* I remember sitting on the couch when I got the news that my grandmother had passed away. She had been in declining health for years, but knowing a person is dying and learning that they have died are two very different things. My now-husband held me and let me cry into his shoulder. He didn't say much, beyond, "I'm sorry;" he simply held me for as long as I wanted to cry.

* I was a graduate instructor at the time. My colleague who taught the same class didn't even ask if I had the emotional energy to do the prep work that week. She simply handed me her lesson plan. I was so grateful.

Worst thing someone did or said:

I was very fortunate that nobody offered me the well-intentioned sorts of silver-lining words that rarely help a person in mourning. Nobody asked if she had lived a long time or whether she was in good health toward the end. Such questions seem designed to make the listener, rather than the griever, feel better.

Advice for someone going through a similar experience:

As much as you feel able, talk about the person who has died. Talk about the good moments and the bad. For over a year after she died, I found myself telling little stories to friends and family. I spoke more about her in the year after she died than in the previous year. I needed to talk and remember, and I was grateful to those who listened.

Advice for those surrounding the bereaved:

* Listen if and when the person in mourning wants to be listened to.
* Offer to help in whatever way you can. Perhaps it's bringing a meal or cutting the grass or lightening a colleague's workload (if possible). Don't be afraid to offer this help even if a month or more has passed.
* Understand that grief lasts far longer than the few days' bereavement leave a person might be given at work. Grief lasts as long as it lasts, and it changes as it goes. Don't be afraid to ask the mourner how they are doing, even long after the fact.

Loss at a Tender Age

Cherry Plum Blossom

| Welton B. Marsland |

The tall eucalyptus trees that had stood there for decades still kept guard over their patch of earth. But in my parents' backyard, the cherry plum ruled supreme. The biggest and most climbable tree, its age was always easy to calculate. Dad had planted it the same month that my older sister was born—so it was the same age as Norma.

There were big age gaps between the children in my family. By the time I—the baby—came along, my siblings were practically all adults. So, I grew up with the life of an only child. The house, the pets, the property, and the parents were all mine. The dog apart, the cherry plum tree was my best friend. Its branches were sturdy and surprisingly smooth. It provided shade and bore delicious fruit. Every summer found me in its arms, living on the cool, sweet flesh of its offspring.

Though just a child, I could see how entwined the cherry plum and my sister, Norma, were in my parents' eyes. Both were a point of pride; both were a source of great beauty. Every spring, delicate white blossoms showered our backyard. Come summer, there was cherry plum jam, stewed cherry plums, cherry plum pie. When visitors complimented Dad on the beauty of his eldest daughter and his garden, they always singled out the cherry plum for special attention.

"Aye," Dad would reply dryly. "And it's the same age as our Norma. Planted it same month she were born. Healthiest, loveliest tree on the land."

For all its closeness to my family, the cherry plum was oblivious to our conversation that summer and the talk beneath its shade revolved around an awful word: cancer. Unlike the rest of us, the tree never drooped its head or sighed or cried at night or slammed doors over and over in anger.

Like Norma, the cherry plum tree seemed undeserving of misfortune or heartache. Yet, within a year of my sister's diagnosis, the tree was beset by a rotting disease. My father, never a very demonstrative man, stormed into the kitchen one night in tears, swearing.

"That shit of a tree, that bloody cherry plum. There's wood rot in its bloody trunk!"

The cherry plum couldn't have understood the anger and hurt that drove my Dad as he hacked at its lower branches with a handsaw. He couldn't bring himself to throw the off-cuts on the incinerator, so my Mum lugged the discarded limbs to their funeral pyre.

Thanks to Dad's radical surgery, the cherry plum tree still stands proud and fruitful in my parents' backyard. Visitors still compliment its beauty. Mum still makes jam.

My sister's radical surgery, however, was not so successful. The week we buried her, the white cherry plum blossoms came out early.

Dedicated to Norma and Alan and Phil

Best thing someone did or said:
Sensing when I needed time alone to process, when I needed some quiet company, and when I really, really needed some very rowdy company indeed.

Worst thing someone did or said:
Let's just say clichés don't ever really help anybody.

Advice for someone going through a similar experience:
Your sense of humor will get you through more than you know.

Advice for those surrounding the bereaved:
It's okay to say, "I don't know what to say."

Big Mountain, Big Ditch

| Ava Green |

One night, my dad came into my room when I was maybe nine. He sat down on the bed with me and turned on the radio. "Lullaby," by Billy Joel was playing. He said, "Listen to this song, Ava. This is a good song." In silence, we sat and listened to the perfect, mournful, loving words.

This is how my dad said good-bye to me, although I didn't know it at the time.

No.

I did.

A strange thing happened after my father died. I suddenly had a completely different understanding of the world than all the kids around me. Already a somewhat shy, awkward girl, I was completely stripped of my ability to relate to anyone. Their worries were not my worries. Their interests (scrunchies, boys, MTV) were not worth my time or consideration.

After the death of my father, I was no longer just another anonymous fifth grade girl. I was suddenly center stage. I was gawked at, everyone falling silent when I walked by. My sadness was frightening. If my dad could just suddenly die, who's to say theirs couldn't either? The nightmare their innocent hearts had never even imagined was my tragic reality. It scared them.

At ten years old, I adopted a somewhat fatalistic and seize-the-moment philosophy. I could have written a brilliant manifesto on the meaning of life, of embracing each precious moment because it could all be snatched away, easy as the wind blows. I could articulate this eloquently and did to my friend Serena. This dear friend, with never an ounce of judgment, was just all listening and love. I was all carpe diem without ever having seen *Dead Poets Society*.

When I did finally see that movie, I cried my eyes out and felt it affirmed my whole life. "This life is fleeting, we must seize the day." I would say these words, but not from a place of peace and love of precious life. I was scared to death. Everything can end, and everything will.

The depths of my sadness and helplessness defy words. I was suddenly unprotected. Exposed. Vulnerable. A little girl without her dad has no warrior. No hero.

It was winter when he died. It was gray when we had to figure out what it meant that he was gone. It was then that I grew up.

Dedicated to Sara, for staying the same

Best thing someone did or said:
My best friend never speculated how she would feel if her parent died. She never made a judgment or gasped or tried to relate. She just listened.

Worst thing someone did or said:
* The one that sticks out as the true worst was, "I wouldn't be able to make it if my dad died." This comment, which I heard more than once, filled me with guilt, as though I was some hardened, heartless person who didn't love my father as much as these kids loved theirs. As though the pain of losing their father would have killed them, but I didn't love mine enough for it to kill me.
* I also remember being very angry anytime someone said, "I'm sorry." As though it was their fault or they had some control over it all. It was usually (and still is occasionally) accompanied by a very sad face. Eventually, I came to accept that those two words were not meant literally. I got over it.

Advice for someone going through a similar experience:
Find the right setting to talk about it. Perhaps a support group so you don't feel isolated. The social isolation and inability to find people who could relate to what I was going through was a huge challenge for me.

Advice for those surrounding the bereaved:

* For newly bereaved parents, don't shut down. Let the grief out; share it with other family members. Hiding the sadness only magnifies it. Show your children that it's okay to express sadness by expressing your own sadness. Don't just tell them it's okay to talk about their feelings.

* For those around a grieving person, if you want to provide relief, treat them normally. Ask outright, "How ya' doing about your dad?" in a normal voice, unafraid of the subject, unafraid of the answer.

Spirits Float

| Jessica Melene |

Where is she?
She is not here
But maybe she is in the sunrise
In the wind that lifts spirits
In the sun that burns
Under the birds that caress the sky
In the falling leaves
Perhaps she is in the sunset
In the crescent moon's radiance
In the pieces of dust illuminating us
In the emerald eyes of the hyena
She's there
She is everywhere but here
And she has my heart

In memory of my one and only mother,
Olga Nyuiadzi (1965-2012)

Best thing someone did or said:
A friend once told me, "No matter how you feel, remember that your body cannot live without your soul. You might want to join her right now wherever she is, but she definitely wants you to stay here and let your soul shine."

Worst thing someone did or said:
One of my teachers told my entire grade about my parental situation in order to justify my numerous absences. At sixteen, knowing that everyone knew made it even harder for me to return to school.

Advice for someone going through a similar experience:

* If there is time, push through your pain and get every single thing you want to say to this person out of your system. Apologize to them. Thank them. Praise them. Everything.

* It will hurt . . . a year from now. Even if you're not in a better place, you will have made it through in an entire year. There's nothing that shows more appreciation to your loved one than that.

(continued on next page)

(continued from previous page)

Advice for those surrounding the bereaved:

* The people who helped me the most were the people who didn't say much at all.
* If they stop talking to you for one reason or another, be forgiving and let them know that you are available when they feel ready to talk. Remind them of their goals. Protect them. Most of all be there for them, even if all the time you spend together is clouded with the weight of silence and sorrow. Just hold their hand and carry that weight with them.

My Grandpa

| Adam L. |

My Grandpa had perfectly white
teeth at the age of 60
or so—I don't really
know—when mine weren't even
adult yet. That was pretty much
all I could remember when he
died.

Nothing was different
except I saw Grandma shed tears
for the first time as we walked to the stage
where he lay in a wooden case
surrounded by real flowers. The whole time
I thought the carnations weren't as white as
his teeth. He's in a better place,
Mom was telling me, so I made a note
to try sleeping in the wooden wardrobe
when we got home.

When Mom and Dad found me
one night, alone in the darkness
of their chifforobe, they startled. Dad said, Stop
playing a fool, and walked away;
Mom gave apologetic eyes.
I didn't understand much then
and even now I don't. But
back in my room, I couldn't stop
hoping they had done the same
to my Grandpa, and that he would
go back to his own bed.

In memory of my Grandpa (2005)

Best thing someone did or said:

My parents are divorced and live in different counties. My grandpa's death was what brought the family together again. I was too young to understand loss, and what I sought then was comfort. After the wake, I stayed with my mom (whom I hadn't seen for years) for about a month and that gave me the care I yearned for and needed.

Worst thing someone did or said:

"You didn't know him."

Advice for someone going through a similar experience:

* You will never "know" them, but you can make an effort to get to know those who do.
* Spending time alone is important. But spending time with others is as important. People will show you, through their own lives, that life still goes on.
* Things will never be the same. Don't make it out to be. Take time to adjust and grieve, but understand also that you are in a new stage of life. Different events and challenges will come. Embrace and experience them. That is what you can give back to the person you have lost.

(continued on next page)

(continued from previous page)

Advice for those surrounding the bereaved:

* A grieving individual might feel especially lonely and helpless. So, offer support with your presence. Being there physically will assure them (and you) that help is available should they want it. You might not even have to do anything. Sometimes, knowing someone is there for them is enough.

* Make sure they don't blame themselves for the death.

* Give them something simple or familiar to do; temporary distraction can help.

Wish List

| Alison Nelson |

Last Will and Christmas presents—
She made sure her shopping was done early.

I rode plush, in the back seat of our
gray Riviera, my ears wrapped
in headphones, listening to my Hallmark tape
—*Elvis's Country Christmas*—over and over.
'Tis the season to be jolly, after all,
and my faith was piled higher
than the banks of snow in the hospital parking lot.

But inside it was harder
to remember, when I had to look at my big sister,
propped up and puffy-faced in her hospital bed,
her pale blue slippers too tight
around her feet. And when she knew
we were there she tried to stretch out
a yellow-cheeked smile.
"Merry Christmas!"

we yelled over the cancer.
Because the cancer was loud and ugly
and deafened her ears.
So I strung up Christmas cards,
made a construction paper sunshine
and hung it on her window.
"To brighten your room," I said.

Now, I wish I could have told her
something, anything—
that I finally passed my driver's test,
that I hated Algebra, that I didn't know
how to say, that I couldn't say,
Good-bye.

Across the hall,
A lady cried through her oxygen mask
sounding low and long and mournful —
again and again.

Outside—the cold December air
helped to freeze my resolve.
In my ears, Elvis promised,
"I'll be home for Christmas . . ."
over and over.

Dedicated to my sister,
Ann Stevens Edwards (1964-1990)

Best thing someone did or said:
I was only sixteen when my sister died, so feeling a little awkward was a normal thing. But the day of my sister's funeral, I remember standing in the back of her church, waiting for my family, feeling very lonely and out of place. A woman approached, put her arm around me and said simply, "I'm just going to stand here with you." I can remember the relief I felt at the kindness of this stranger, just being there with me as I fought back tears. I have no idea who she was, and to this day I have wondered if perhaps she was an "angel unawares" (Hebrews 13:2). Whether a real angel or not, she certainly was like an angel to me that day, bringing peace and comfort when I needed it most.

Worst thing someone did or said:
"You'll see her again someday" or "We know she is in a better place." Early on, this was not very comforting to me—though it is now. I remember thinking that I should be more comforted by my faith, but at that time I wasn't.

Advice for someone going through a similar experience:
  * For me, getting back to a normal routine and feeling secure in my surroundings was the most comforting thing.

(continued on next page)

(continued from previous page)

 * Don't think you should be feeling one thing or another. If you aren't feeling sad at a particular moment, that is okay. It doesn't mean that you love the person who died any less or that they weren't important to you.
 * Realize that the way you process your grief as a teenager may be different than when you are an adult. I feel like I went through a second grieving period as an adult, although not as intense as the first.

Advice for those surrounding the bereaved:

 * To parents of a teenager experiencing grief over the loss of a sibling: make sure the teen doesn't feel like they have to take care of the parent or be "good."
 * Provide the teenager with opportunities to talk to people outside the family, if they feel the need (e.g., school counselor, pastor, therapist, trusted friends).

Persistent Loss

Manhood Dreams

| Len Lawson |

He died when I was a boy.

Decades later, I still experience his death in dreams, but in each, I am a grown man. In one, I run away from my family and do not attend the funeral. During their worship service, I hide in a different church where no one knows or recognizes me. Eventually friends and family find me there. Was I a man or still just a boy?

In another dream, a man-sized me is in the middle of a little league baseball game. I round second base to make a triple, but the throw to third stops my progress. Every kid on the field and both coaches converge to tag me out in a rundown. When they finally do, I look to the stands searching for Daddy. He isn't there. To me, I was still just a boy.

I am also a man in a dream where I am driving Daddy's big, bright red Ford pick-up. Where its proportions dwarfed me as a kid, now it fits just right, with my hands on the steering wheel and him beside me in the passenger seat. We pull into a gas station and, when two men come up to service our vehicle, we get out of the truck. Together, we stare into an open frontier that looks like one of those 1940s, picturesque movie scenes. We just stand there quietly, two men side by side. It is the best moment of my life—in a dream.

Today, I tended my father's gravesite. We had a good conversation. I said, "You were a better man than I could ever hope to be. You provided for a family and still cared for your elderly mother after her husband's death. You were a dad to sons, nephews, and fathers. I am not yet a man. When I die, I want to be buried right beside you so that you can finish teaching me."

Then, I asked why he keeps showing up in my dreams. His response was the same as always: no answer. In death as in life, his presence was enough.

Twenty-five years later I still cry about it—damn cigarettes, damn beer, damn diabetes.

At some point, my manhood will stop dreaming of being a boy and will become a man. My manhood has dreams like I do. Both of us want men we cannot have.

In memory of my father,
Lenord Lawson, Sr. (1953-1992)

Best thing someone did or said:
* A man recorded a wrestling pay-per-view event for me because he knew my dad loved pro wrestling. I did, too.
* Days after my father's passing, my uncle took me for a one-mile walk, consoling me as I cried and hugged him around his waist the entire way.
* My eighth grade classmates all signed a card for me when I returned to school.

Worst thing someone did or said:
I slept in the same bed with my sister the night after the funeral. I moaned through tears, "Wanda, he's never coming back . . ." She told me to just go to sleep. But I know she was grieving, too.

Advice for someone going through a similar experience:
* Cherish the best memories you had with the deceased.
* Remember things they did to make you laugh.
* Continue to discuss them with others to keep their legacy alive.

Advice for those surrounding the bereaved:
* Do not force an individual either to grieve or to stop grieving.
* Share your best memories of the deceased with the grieving individual.
* Use affection (i.e., hugs) to help the individual through the process—even without saying anything.

Reflections from the Wall

| Robert B. Robeson |

"All these were glorious in their time, each
illustrious in his day . . . All these are buried
in peace, but their name lives on and on."
—*Ecclesiasticus,* Chapter 44

My palms started to sweat and my throat tightened and became
dry as I neared the end of an extended odyssey to say good-
bye to some gallant and special friends, who'd been waiting
patiently for over five years to have me drop by. The last time
I'd seen them was eighteen years before as a helicopter medical evacuation pilot in South Vietnam, with dead and wounded
overflowing my aircraft. On this day in our nation's capital,
though, I was merely a forty-five-year-old soldier, just days
from a military retirement.

Most walls keep us apart, but the Vietnam Veterans Memorial had drawn me from Nebraska like steel filings to a magnet . .
. a force tugging me home. As I approached the twin black granite scrolls that gracefully join in the center of a carpet of green
in a peaceful corner of the Mall, I was awestruck. Nearly two
decades after my initial combat involvement, I knew that what-

ever the people whose names had been grit-blasted into that wall and I had once been to each other, we still were. We all share the unbearable grief of our Vietnam involvement . . . the brevity of human life in time of war . . . any war.

Memories of combat and the personalities involved work like a yo-yo. You can watch them fall away toward the end of the string, but they never die there. They merely sleep. The point in time always arrives when, in a moment of reflection, they roll back up into your hand. As long as they are tied to your life and soul in this manner, they will keep returning to your thoughts on a regular basis . . . like a boomerang or the swallows to Capistrano.

Passersby whispered, trying not to disturb the tranquility of the setting or those who stood transfixed before this commanding stone presence. My fingers instinctively reached out to softly trace the names of those I'd known and the many I'd carried, like Captain John R. Hill, a friend still missing in action. His name is located in the center of panel 11 west, on line 58.

All the names of those who lost their lives or remain missing are inscribed on the mirror-like surfaces of these V-shaped, brooding black walls whose panels are as flat as still water. The largest panels have 137 lines of names; the shortest have one line.

The average age of a soldier in this conflict was nineteen, barely out of high school. All of them gave up two lives—the one they were living and the one they would have lived. My hair contains a bit of gray now, and I've put on some weight. But none of these Americans ever grew old. Nor did they have to deal with physical or mental disfigurement . . . Agent Orange . . . flashbacks. They discovered that life is as uncertain as the morning fog. Now you see it. Soon it's gone. For them, there's nothing left to worry about. Unlike those who remain, they do not cry or feel anger or churn with survivor's guilt.

Reflections from the Wall are like laser beams to the heart. The list begins in the center of the memorial and ends in the center. As you read the inscribed names, you see yourself reflected in the granite. Regardless which angle you view it from, you are looking at yourself through the names of the dead. You are a part of it. The Wall and those whose names appear on it, in turn, will always be a part of us. When it rains, all of the names disappear because water makes the etched portions of the stone take on the same color as its polished surface. When we weep, the names are not easily seen, either.

The Wall is where all 58,000-plus of these American heroes have been symbolically buried. Their final curtain has been lowered in a dignified manner. I'll be forever grateful for this respectful act of human decency.

Good-bye, my friends. Get some rest. You've earned it. How fortunate we are to have had you serve America. How fortunate I am to have known so many of you.

Dedicated to Capt. John R. Hill (U.S. Army Aviation)
Missing in action on April 27, 1970

Best thing someone did or said:
"Every combat veteran has to come to terms with the trauma of their war involvement. After a number of years, you'll learn that it's all right to have survived when so many others didn't. Bonus time and opportunities have been allocated to you, for some reason, and your responsibility is to be wise in their use. And you will never forget those who have suffered so long from the devastation of Vietnam or who have given their all for others at such a young age."

Worst thing someone did or said:
"You were crazy for having volunteered for Vietnam."

Advice for someone going through a similar experience:
   * Ignore negative comments from anyone who never served in Vietnam or who has never been in combat. They have no idea what the experience was like or what you went through.
   * As most theatergoers know, at the end of *Hamlet* the stage is littered with dead bodies. Yet some of the characters are still alive. And life must go on.

Advice for those surrounding the bereaved:
   * Listen to them in silence.
   * Don't give advice unless asked.
   * Pray for them.

Time

| Kate Redderson-Lear |

It's the moving on that gets us.

The grief is one thing. It's appropriate. Understandable. But the realization that you've forgotten, that for even a moment the grief has lifted, is almost worse because with the return of the fist around your heart comes the weight of guilt. You don't want to move on. You don't want to be happy. You don't want the pain to go away. That would be betrayal of the worst kind.

The first forgetting and crush of remembrance is the hardest. The moments to follow will be bad, yes, nearly unbearable. But the first time, the visceral realization that you're capable of forgetting, even for a second, knocks you off your feet and twists everything you thought you knew about yourself. The moments after that can be strong and terrible, but they're merely echoes of that first wrench. Then, quickly, you discover that even that feeling of guilt has a time limit.

Humans adapt, after all. It's how we survive. We keep going. The holes in our hearts are patched over. Not healed, maybe, but the wound grows old, the deep scar fades. However often we try to rip it back open, make ourselves feel that pain, we get used to it eventually.

We will move on. We will forget the little things, think less often of the big things. It is a mercy and a curse. We don't want to forget. We don't want to remember that we can forget. That our lives are so impermanent. We want to think our legacy will last forever.

But this is the inevitable curse and mercy of time: it goes on. Always. Inexorably. It tears us apart and makes life bearable, breaking and healing our hearts simultaneously.

Best thing someone did or said:
The best thing anyone did for me during the grieving period was take me out to eat several times a week with zero pressure to talk about how I was feeling. Beforehand, this friend said flat out that he would be happy to talk, but that if I didn't feel like it he would be happy to sit and stare at the table with me. Those were possibly the most comforting meals I had during that time. So many people were asking me how I felt and if I was okay, and I didn't know how to answer any of them. So to sit with someone and just know they cared, without any questions or expectations, felt like a miracle. Also, since I wasn't eating much at that point, going out to eat kept me healthy.

Worst thing someone did or said:
The worst thing someone said to me during the grieving period was, "Well, life isn't fair; this kind of thing happens every day. You'll be okay." I already knew that life wasn't fair, and that death happens far too often. That didn't make my friend's death any less important to me, and although I'm sure that person meant to be comforting, I didn't actually want to be okay—I wanted to properly mourn the amazing and beautiful person my friend was.

Advice for someone going through a similar experience:
* Be mindful of your own feelings, and let yourself feel them. If you're angry, think about why. If you laugh at a memory of something they did, enjoy the memory, and don't squash the laugh.

* Don't think too much about how you should be feeling, especially compared to other people. Concentrate on how you actually feel.
* Get out. Get exercise. Do it in a place you'll be able to relax or clear your mind, not in your house. It'll help you sleep, it'll keep your appetite up and, possibly most important, it will remind you there's still a world out there.

Advice for someone going through a similar experience:
* Make sure they know you care about them and you're there if they need to talk, but don't pressure them to speak.
* Offer to take them places or to do things that remind them there is still a world out there and they are still very much a part of it.

Teresa's Russet Cowgirl Boots

| E. G. Moore |

Never before had I heard Rusty whinny so pitifully. Normally, my sister Teresa's horse was full of attitude and rebellion. But the afternoon of June 1, 2006, he bowed his head low and haunted the gate like a ghost. Somehow, he sensed Teresa's death.

Earlier that day Teresa's best friend, Amanda, had taken her for a four-wheeler ride up a dirt road a half a mile from our home in the eastern hills of Hayfork, California. On the way back, Amanda skidded on loose rock and the vehicle careened down an embankment, smashing my sister against a tree. Despite protective gear, Teresa's small frame took a hit that caused fatal internal bleeding. When my family received the autopsy and alcohol reports twenty-four hours later, the results shocked us. Teresa liked to drink occasionally, as did Amanda, and all of us assumed that when one drank, the other partook as well. But Teresa's blood came back clean, while Amanda's alcohol level was illegal. The state charged her with manslaughter, rocking the Hayfork community as people debated whether to blame Amanda for Teresa's death or to support her as she writhed in guilt for killing her best friend.

Teresa embodied the kind of country teen who lived for the heat of the day and the love of her animals. Absent a school project or things to gossip about with her friends, she stayed busy mucking out pens or taking Rusty for a ride. She always sported blue jeans, a plain spaghetti strap tank, a brightly colored visor, and her cherished pair of russet cowgirl boots. While Rusty dominated her animal world, Teresa successfully cajoled our parents to take in two 4H steers, a 4H pig, a mutt named Cody, and her purebred chocolate lab, Jake. Gradually, she built a small hobby farm on my parents' land. Every pet, even my mom's two cranky old tomcats, adored her.

Now, as I stood on the family porch watching Cody and Jake pace in the eastern pasture, I realized it wasn't just Rusty who sensed my baby sister's absence. Dad had penned the dogs so they wouldn't bother the family friends, classmates of Teresa, and Hayfork High School teachers flowing through our house to offer their condolences. My parents embraced all the help and love. I, on the other hand, ached for solitude and prayer. *Days like this were her favorite,* I thought as sobs bubbled up in my chest.

Life carried on, and with it joy reawakened, a feeling no one expects to experience again when they miss a loved one. Losing my sister forced me to face that the love I felt for my best friend, Nolan, was far more than platonic. Seven months after Teresa passed, Nolan and I exchanged vows and rings. Then we conceived and delivered two beautiful daughters, Brylie, now seven, and Mikayla, four. After the US Navy decided to relocate Nolan's mechanic skills, our absence opened the door for several of my childhood friends and their children to draw closer to my mother. While the distance strained my own relationship with my parents, it created the space I needed to deal with my own grief. From the day of Brylie's birth, my mom and dad had been connecting her every mannerism and experience to Teresa's childhood. It was driving me crazy.

One Sunday, as Mom and I chatted on the phone, she asked me how I would feel about them selling Rusty. "He won't let me ride him," she said. "And he is still so young. He deserves to be in a place where he will be taken care of and ridden more often."

I gave my blessing for the sale, then got off the phone quickly and burst into tears. Deep down, I recognized that this decision was part of my parents' healing process. But for me, Rusty and the other farm critters represented Teresa's lingering presence among us. Getting rid of Rusty restarted the anguish of loss in my soul.

A month later, I logged onto Facebook and noticed a post by one of my friends, whom Mom dotes on like a daughter. "Jake is so happy to be here and Ashlyn loves giving him hugs and kisses. His tail won't stop wagging!" Resisting the urge to comment or call my mom in a rage, I talked to my husband and prayed. When Mom phoned a week later, I tried—and failed—to sound casual as I mentioned that I'd learned, via a Facebook post no less, that she'd given away Teresa's beloved dog. "You should have told me!"

"We are sorry," she replied. "We didn't think it would affect you like this."

During subsequent trips home, I noticed other things missing. A saddle. A piece of clothing. With each new discovery, my heart proved it is in fact a muscle, breaking down in discomfort and growing stronger than before. Looking back now, I see the hypocrisy of judging my parents' grief journey. We each handle loss in our own way. They needed to dispose; I needed to cling.

On my most recent visit, our entire clan finally relaxed, subconsciously closing the gaps Teresa and her things had created in the family circle. The only beast left on my parents' property, a young, male feline, proudly dropped a fresh-killed mole at Mom's feet. Our girls luxuriated in Grandma and Grandpa's attention. We smoothed into the pleasure of being a family again.

In Teresa's old bedroom, Dad had stacked a half dozen boxes that awaited my attention. Mom instructed me to take anything I wanted; she planned to donate the rest. Near the bottom of the last box, my hands brushed tough leather. My sister's russet cowgirl boots. Mom and I exchanged smiles without tears for the first time since Teresa left us. "Thank you," I whispered to the photo of Teresa hanging on the wall. "These are staying in the family."

Though the twin pastures on my parents' property now sit empty, those well-worn boots constantly remind me of Teresa's soft and smiling face. People say time is a great physician, but Nolan and I plan to use it as a stepping-stone. Our hope is to build a small farm of our own when Nolan leaves the Navy life behind. We will use it to teach our girls not only about hard work and the joy of working the land, but also about the aunt who delights in them from heaven. One thing I know for certain: both of Teresa's nieces will wear her boots.

In memory of my sister,
Teresa Kay Brown (1989-2006)

Best thing someone did or said:
My friend Tyler pushed me on a tire swing and let me cry, knowing that words wouldn't do any good.

Worst thing someone did or said:
Someone told me I was being selfish by not grieving with the rest of my family.

Advice for someone going through a similar experience:
Don't isolate yourself all the time. It's okay to be alone, but always, always make time to be with others to be held or to cry with them. There's comfort in the presence of others.

Advice for those surrounding the bereaved:
Don't try to force people to grieve a certain way. Encourage them to do whatever helps them through it. Even if you don't understand, support them in their weirdness anyway. They'll remember your loving actions with gratitude.

Memory Album

| Lisa Siedt |

As we drove to meet our youngest daughter for breakfast near her Canadian university before heading home to the States, home to another year apart, my mind flipped through my memory album and stopped at an image of her as a newborn. She is screaming and waving a fist at the injustice of being dragged from her warm "bed" into the cold surgical suite. Though the image is careworn and faded, it still feels fresh. Wasn't that just yesterday?

And wasn't it just yesterday that I held our firstborn, our son, as his life slipped away? How fragile everything felt back then. How fragile everything truly is.

I do not consider myself a brave person. I have more phobias than I care to admit. But my largest fear, the fear of losing a loved one is not a phobia. It's a rational fear, born of experience. I've had seven pregnancies. Out of all those, only two daughters lived.

I cannot tell you where I found the courage to attempt the pregnancy that gave birth to our eldest daughter. Ray and I were on the healing side of two miscarriages, just months apart, when we watched our son live his short, precious life of thirty hours. Could we really do this again after witnessing the inconceivable: a child of ours leaving this world before we did?

Still, I wanted a child desperately; down to my core, I wanted a child. I decided I was not going to let my fear of another loss, another profound grief, keep me from trying again. Fairy tales would have us believe that Fate would perform penance and give us a smooth sail through this next pregnancy. It was not to be.

Consigned to continuous bed rest, I had way too much time for my favorite pastime: worrying. I kept a journal of doctor visits, mile markers of the pregnancy, sonogram snapshots, and my thoughts for my new baby. My eldest daughter now has custody of this journal. She told me my entries to her make her feel that I was encouraging her to be born safely, coaxing her to continue the pregnancy until the time was right. I like thinking of my entries this way. At the time, the journal was simply my last grasp at sanity.

One of my most joyous moments in life was hearing my daughter emit her first cry. In memory, I carry a photograph of her resting on my chest for the very first time.

I also carry photographs of each of those I lost. These images, embedded forever in my memory, convince me that bravery does not preclude fear. Rather, bravery is doing the right thing in spite of fear. Each of my photographs of loss has a permanent a place in my mind, heart, and soul. They remind me daily how priceless my loved ones are to me. They remind me that being brave and fighting through my fear was completely and utterly worth it.

*Dedicated to my husband, Ray Siedt,
who traveled this path with me*

Best thing someone did or said:

My mother and my brother were with us while we held our son in his last moments. They didn't say much that I remember, but their presence was and is so very important to me.

Worst thing someone did or said:

"You can always have another baby." How can you possibly know whether or not that is true?

Advice for someone going through a similar experience:

* Don't trick yourself into thinking that if you ignore the pain it will go away. Time does *not* heal all pain. You have to experience it in order to find a way to live with it.
* Remember that your spouse is a separate person. Even if they do not seem as sad as you, your spouse is still grieving.

Advice for those surrounding the bereaved:

Everyone grieves in their own way and time. You are not required to fix this. You cannot. Patience is all that is required. Just be there.

Waiting on the Bus

| Denise Grier |

I hear a cheerful shout and pull back the curtain.
Like a spy, I watch him.
He's waiting for the bus. Fine!

The bus stop is on the corner, next
to my bedroom window.
Dejected is the spy—yes, I— though glorious
is the morning sunlight filtering
through the branches of the trees outside
my cozy apartment.

He's crazy. He's living
in the past. The old fool rubs
his hands together, takes
an invisible baseball bat,
lovingly lays it across his shoulder,
talks to a coach only he sees, waiting
on a ghost pitcher, a fast ball
from 40 years ago.

While he, this ragged stranger, is waiting
for the bus that will take him
to the shelter, or the halfway house,
or maybe even to his family,
to a child or a woman who loves him,

I wait for a bus,
the one I've been waiting
on for a year,

the one that will take
me to the end of my life,
my child, an athlete,
his suicide my ticket.

I smile, a forgotten feeling,
as the stranger,
unaware of me watching,
changes sports, cheering.
Years fall away as he jumps
his invisible basketball sailing
through the crisp morning air.

Dedicated to Clint

Best thing someone did or said:
"I can't imagine how you feel."

Worst thing someone did or said:
"He's in a better place."

Advice for someone going through a similar situation:
- * Understand that you are not yourself and won't be for some time.
- * Give yourself a break, pamper yourself, and love yourself.
- * Let that little voice that says, "Time heals," have some say; even though you won't believe it, it is true.

Advice for those surrounding the bereaved:
Don't say you understand or that the person is in a better place. Just be there for them and listen. Don't push, but don't abandon.

Complicated Loss

Dry Heaves

| Skot Kortrijk |

It's the middle of the night, and I'm on the last page or so of *Damien* by Hermann Hesse. Phone rings. It's my mom.

"Hey," I say. "What's up?"

She tells me something is going on in Guerneville. My dad threatened her. Got out one of the guns. She sounds really shaken. He just snapped. Said he's been saving three bullets, and one of them has her name on it. He's in the house with the gun out, and the bullets. He showed her the bullet. The police are on their way over. She and Jennifer got out of the house as fast as they could and went across the street to the sheriff's office. Jennifer doesn't even have any shoes on.

"You know this isn't going to end in a good way, right, Skot?"

"I know . . . Fuck . . . I know."

"I gotta go. They've got us in a holding cell on the far end of the building. I don't think I'm supposed to be calling you right now. I'll call you as soon as I can."

I go outside. Light a cigarette. Pace back and forth.

"Fuck."

My roommate, James, comes outside, or maybe he's inside, I don't remember. I tell him what's going on. His girlfriend works as a police dispatcher. Maybe she can get some more information. He calls her on the phone, then starts asking me a bunch of questions about what the address is, how do you spell my mom's name, all that. I go back outside and sit down and stare at the fire in the fire pit.

It starts raining.

I try calling my dad, but it goes straight to voicemail. I don't leave a message.

I don't hear anything back from my mom. James says it was just a lights and sirens call. No fatalities. I tell him if he hears any different, I don't want to hear it from him. That would be a fucked up way to find out. I'd rather hear it from my mom.

I go to bed. Last thing I remember hearing that night is James in his room. "Awwww . . . Fuck."

Phone wakes me. It's my mom. She tells me the news. The police shot him. It's in the newspaper already. She and Jennifer are still in a holding cell. She found out from my Uncle Dino. He saw it on the news and called her to find out what was going on. Nobody has told her anything.

"Where are you guys now? Should I come to Guerneville? What do I do?"

"They're taking us to Petaluma to talk to an investigator. I don't know how long that's going to take."

We start to make a plan. Then she has to go again. She'll call later with more information.

I go outside and start a fire in the fire pit. I don't know what else to do. I just start a fire and stare at it.

It feels like I'm going to start crying. My dad is dead. The feeling doesn't come out as tears. It gets choked back in my throat. It's like a dry heave. It's a retch.

"Fuck."

Dedicated to Wayne Courtright Jr.

Best thing someone did or said:
People didn't really know how to react when I told them what happened to my father, and I didn't really know what to do either. I appreciated the friends and family who didn't pressure me with too many questions right away. They let me get my thoughts together and work through my feelings at my own pace.

Worst thing someone did or said:
I got fired from my job after taking time off to be with my family. And since I lived and worked at the same place, I was suddenly homeless, unemployed, and grieving at the same time.

Advice for someone going through a similar experience:
Take time to feel your feelings and let them run their course. Some days are going to be pretty difficult, and you might find your thoughts to be unbearable, but just hang in there and hold on to the knowledge that it will get better with time.

Advice for those surrounding the bereaved:
Make yourself available to listen or to help. Just let them know you're there for them when they need you. Don't push too hard to talk about things. Just be there.

A Struggle to Survive

| R. J. Wasser |

Solitude
The cold beneath me
Beneath my feet
Proof enough of the warmth
Fleeting it extends, crawling
Never promised and never concrete
But always welcome, all the same
This thing is anything but a dream
To me it seems life is but a game
Never concede, forever forward
One last try,
Into the breach dear friends
Once more
I reach up to the heavens
I grasp for glory
Once more
A struggle to survive
Never ending

*Dedicated to PFC Clinton Springer and
all my other Brothers in Arms*

Best thing someone did or said:
A dear friend gave me a plaque with this old Irish blessing inscribed on it:

"MAY THE ROAD RISE UP TO MEET YOU.
MAY THE WIND ALWAYS BE AT YOUR BACK.
MAY THE SUN SHINE WARM UPON YOUR FACE,
AND RAINS FALL SOFT UPON YOUR FIELDS.
AND UNTIL WE MEET AGAIN,
MAY GOD HOLD YOU IN THE PALM OF HIS HAND."

Worst thing someone did or said:
People who asked me if I had emotional problems, because they couldn't understand why I was reacting like I was.

Advice for someone going through a similar experience:
Nothing can replace what you've lost or make amends for what you've been through, but you have to know that there is somebody out there who understands what you're going through and will be there for you.

Advice for those surrounding the bereaved:
While it might seem like you need to pay constant attention to that person (and you very well may have to), remember that he's still a normal person, and normal people need space.

Loss Upon Loss Upon Loss

| Margaret Roberts |

*This is what I wrote when, fourteen years into our marriage, I
lost my husband to alcohol.*

The saddest thing of all
is that he was one thing in my mind
and another thing entirely
in reality.

It was that way for him, too,
in relation to me.
I never really loved *him*,
and he never really loved *me*.

Most of us do that, I think.
We build fantasies in our minds
about who people are
and we fall in love
with those phantoms.

I still do it.
I'm still in love with the phantom
I made of him.
The man who remains?
He terrifies me.

This is what I wrote when I lost him again three years later, this time because I left him.

It's always there, waiting,
you know?
Without any warning, my thoughts will turn
a certain way—just a slight turn —
it doesn't take much . . .

And suddenly,
my heart is aching,
my stomach is hollow
and life has become utterly meaningless.

Such a small movement, that turn,
for such a huge change—
from life
to annihilation.

He thinks I won't go through this.
He's wrong.

This is what I wrote years after I lost him—forever—to suicide.

He doesn't think anymore
because he shot a bullet into his brain.

Actually, through it,
with great precision and knowledge
and forethought.
He didn't want to be get caught again
and be trapped by society's laws and rules and institutions.
He was afraid that would happen again
because it happened a year earlier
when I left him.

So, you know I think I killed him, right?
Yes.
Right.

The days go by;
they have gone by.
They've added up to months and years.

Each moment.
Each decision.
Each thought.
Each action.
Each feeling.
All have added up,
making me into someone who
is no longer the same person who was there
and who left
and who was left.

I've lost a lot—hope most of all.
Now, I live because
I woke up this morning.

Each day
I discover myself
and the choices I can make.
Every now and then,
joy finds me.

Best thing someone did or said:
My mother and brother helped me with some practical matters.

Worst thing someone did or said:
No one wanted to hear me talk about anything.

Advice for someone going through a similar situation:
* Try to find someone compassionate to listen to you.
* Write. Journal about exactly how you feel, no matter how "unacceptable" or contradictory your thoughts and feelings may be.
* Occasionally reread what you wrote.

Advice for those surrounding the bereaved:
* Listen as much as you can bear to.
* Don't assume that because a person is crying they need a hug. Sometimes your presence is enough.
* Don't offer platitudes or solutions. Attentive silence can be enough.

"Go Give Beeps a Kiss Good-bye"

| Rachel White |

My two year old is scared of the gentlest man I've ever known.

My dad enlisted as a Marine in Vietnam. You know it from the bumper sticker and sweatshirts, even if you don't see the baseball cap. Six foot four inches and lean, yet not what you think of when you think of a jarhead. I can't remember him ever raising his voice, except when he would try to roust three teenagers into the car in time for church. "LET'S GO, PEOPLE!" he would holler up the stairs. Even when I sneaked out my bedroom window at three a.m. and he was waiting for me on the porch, he spoke softly. "You might as well come in through the front door." During long car rides, he would tell stories about "the service." His voice is almost gone now, no more stories.

The VA says his disease might be from Agent Orange. It is called progressive supranuclear palsy, or PSP. A cousin to Parkinson's, it's a mean disease. It started killing him a couple years ago. At first, my dad said he felt drunk all the time, couldn't think clearly, and was losing his balance. He fell a couple times.

He also became more impulsive. He often got dizzy on the stairs, but would march up the twelve stone steps in front of my house. STOP! I wanted to yell, like I do at my kids when they get near the road. You could die! But he's a grown man, and my dad.

At Christmastime, he fell down the stairs and broke some bones, spent the holidays in the hospital. We gathered around his bed, trying to be merry, but my mom's tears betrayed us. My other memories of this hospital involve beginnings. When I gave birth. When I came to see my brand new nephews. Now, I saw my father lying pale in the hospital bed, and it hit me that he was dying. I always knew it. But now I saw it when he tried to sit up, and felt it in the tremors when he held my hand.

I don't blame my daughter for being frightened. My dad's spare frame has lost fifty pounds, turned gaunt. When we visit my parents' house, he is usually dozing in the hospital bed set up in the family room because he can't make it up the stairs to his bedroom. He sleeps with his mouth open.

I cover him with a thick blanket whenever I go by; he looks so cold. When I would fall asleep on the couch watching Carol Burnett, he would carry me up to bed, pull my covers up over me. He woke me every morning before school with a gentle shake of my shoulder, and coached every basketball team I was on until junior high. Never missed a game. This is what love looks like.

"Go give Beeps a kiss good-bye," I tell my two year old as we prepare to leave.

My dad is kind and funny at surprising times. He always smiles when he sees the kids, and always reaches out to touch a hand or shoulder. I cannot imagine being scared of so gentle a man. I've never been frightened of him. But I see my daughter's hesitation. So I take her pudgy little hand in mine and together we go into the family-room-turned-hospital-room. We kiss him good-bye.

Dedicated to my dad, Tony Cherry (1945-2014)

Best thing someone did or said:
A friend I hadn't seen in a long time showed up at the funeral. She drove a long way and brought her two young sons. It was unexpected and special.

Worst thing someone did or said:
The worst thing someone can do is nothing. Many people are so scared of death that they hide from it and hide from you. When someone you expect to be there for you isn't, it adds to the loss.

Advice for someone going through a similar experience:
* Surround yourself with people you love and who love you.
* Share happy memories and laugh at silly things your loved one did. Remember.

Advice for those surrounding the bereaved:
Let them grieve on their own schedule and in their own way. Hold their hand and hug them and be there to listen.

A Different Narrative

| Annalyn Randall |

Typically, when people hear about a recent death, they offer pity and apologies. I can understand why this is done. Yet, not all fathers are missed.

When I was thirteen, my father went to prison. At a time when I could have benefited from a father figure, mine was sent away for hurting others. The night my grandmother called to tell us, we thought she was calling to say he was dead. I hadn't seen him for weeks and he had a very weak heart. Much of my childhood had been spent in hospital rooms. When the word "prison" hit my ear, I wanted to burst. I was prepared for an eternal good-bye. Instead, I was given the shame of sharing chromosomes with a rapist.

In coming years, that shame was often tinged with guilt. After all, his blood runs in my veins. Shouldn't I strive to help him rather than try to purge myself of him? Shouldn't I love him solely for playing a part in giving me life? That guilt hardened, settling in the bottom of my belly.

One day, as I sat beside my mother, she turned to me and said, "Your father died this morning."

When loved ones die, we are meant to cry. When there is loss in our lives, we grieve. So, even though I had lost this man many years before his death, I expected to walk the path of a grieving daughter. To find out what I should be doing, I Googled "when your father dies." But as I read blog posts and articles, I began to sense that my relationship with my father absolutely had the right to be treated differently than what was expected. Again, I turned to Google, but I wrote, "when your convict father dies in prison." Nothing. No matter the combination of words I threw at Google, it had nothing for me. My family pestered me to express my feelings, but I genuinely didn't know. What was I supposed to feel?

At the funeral, I felt like a stranger who didn't quite belong. Mourners provided stories of a man I never knew. I told myself, "Allow them to have him the way they do." At the back of the church, a small woman standing next to the picture of my father looked directly at me and said, "As a baby, he used to bring you to visit. You were the light of his world."

I don't know what changed in him. I can't fathom why he showed me nothing but anger as I aged. Much too soon, I lost what should have been protection, wisdom, support, and love. In a pew, holding my mother's hand, I wept for the little girl who grew up fatherless, not for the adult woman who was burying a body.

Every day, we experience loss. Loss of time. Loss of sleep. Loss of memory and youth. But a *great* loss—death—deserves to be treated uniquely. We should open our hearts and our ears to those who are grieving, and leave our assumptions at the door. We should approach death outside of the scripts we know, and let these stories be told in their own way and in their own time.

Dedicated to my grandfather, Robert Randall (1934–2011),
who inspired me to be the best I could be

Best thing someone did or said:
I can't think of kind words from when my father died. However, when my grandmother died, my mother and I spent a lot of time laying around giggling about my grandmother's unruly salt and pepper hair. It truly helped a lot. At the time of her death, I also read *Death is Nothing at All* by Henry Scott Holland. It talks about how the person isn't gone, they've simply stepped into the next room. According to Holland, death is a short goodbye; it is not permanent. He says, "I am but waiting for you, for an interval, very near. Just around the corner." I took that to mean that death is the same good-bye you would give when kissing someone good night. At some point, you see them again. They come back to you. That was what I needed to ease the pain of my grief.

Worst thing someone did or said:
"You were a selfish daughter."

Advice for someone going through a similar experience:
* Give yourself time and freedom to feel everything that you feel.
* Don't allow anyone to tell you how you should feel or react.
* Know that grief doesn't look a certain way.

Advice for those surrounding the bereaved:
* Ask how they feel, and if it's not what you expect, revise your schema.
* Ask if they need anything, and if they don't, give them space. For me, all I wanted was peace, in other words, solitude. It was through quietness and space from others that I found healing.

Unacknowledged Loss

Joey

| Karen Burton |

Googled your name.
Zero hits.
No money trail,
Facebook pics,
email.
Cyber world
provides no record
of short lives.
As if
no information
equals no impact.

But letters etched
in marble,
cold and permanent
Joey

May 24 – June 2, 1993
mark forever
your life,
date the meteor strike.
Nine days
of flash, fire.
Craters carved,
smoking still
after 22 years.

In memory of my son, Joseph Allen Burton (1993)

Best thing someone did or said:
When crying to a friend that I felt that God and my faith had abandoned me, he replied, "It is hard to hear the whispers of God and faith when your soul is screaming in pain. We are listening, even if you can't hear us."

Worst thing someone did or said:
People tried to put a positive spin on my loss. At least . . . you have another son. At least . . . you can have more children. And the worse one of all . . . at least you never brought him home from the hospital, so you didn't get attached.

Advice for someone going through a similar experience:
* Accept your journey as unique, with its own time frame and struggles.
* Tell yourself that it will get better until you finally, one day, believe it.
* Seek out beauty in nature, in art, in music. The beauty will bring you tears of healing.

Advice for those surrounding the bereaved:
* When in doubt, don't say it.
* Your presence is more important than your words.
* Always make your offers of help specific. Never say, "Whatever you need," because that puts the burden on the grieving individual to think about and ask for help.

Again

| E. Buhr |

I sat in my car crying. The phone call had come two hours earlier. A soft voice telling me that, unfortunately, the blood test was negative again. I had failed, again. Two long hours of pretending to listen while staff talked to me. Two long hours of trying to pay attention to forms and emails. My brain felt fuzzy and I found myself frequently taking deep breaths to calm the sob welling up in the back of my throat. Finally the workday had ended and I escaped to my car.

Sobbing in the car was not new. For months, I had sobbed to and from each appointment. Kind people would smile patiently, gently reassure, and then insert, remove, poke, and prod. They were trying to help, and they were incredibly professional. It was not their fault. It was something in me. Something was the matter with me.

In our modern society, women can do anything. We can run triathlons or climb Everest. We can be a surgeon or an entrepreneur. We can drive racecars and fight in wars. At our very core, however, is the ability to grow a baby in our belly. For some reason, a baby did not want to grow in mine. The immense feeling of inadequacy and failure was shocking. Women are supposed to make babies. How could I not do something so basic and natural? Once the self-pitying sobs stopped, I was still. It was time to make a decision.

Adoption is a good choice. Difficult in its own way, but no one sticks you with needles. There are babies all around the world in need of parents who will love and provide for them. I could do that. I could be a mother to someone who needs a mom.

Being childless also has its perks. I could forever sleep in on Saturday mornings if I wanted. My travel plans and evening schedules would never revolve around a child's sleep schedule or soccer game. I liked my life. Why was I trying so hard to alter it?

Either of those choices sounded good to me after three years of endless, all-consuming infertility. Anything to break the cycle of disappointment. I didn't see how I could possibly put myself through the pain and stress and aching sadness again. The frustration of the unknown, the stressful imposition of the precise scheduling, the tentative wonder and hope, the crushing failure, the resulting emptiness. I couldn't possibly be brave enough or crazy enough to submit myself to another round no matter how much I wanted a child.

No matter how much I wanted a child.

Calm now, I picked up the phone to make a call of my own. Tuesday at 8:15 a.m. we would start trying, again.

Best thing someone did or said:
While we were going through IVF, a friend commented one afternoon that people tend to share their happy moments with friends and family, but not their hard moments. She said that it is when we are going through a hard time that we most need our loved ones. This wise thought encouraged me to be more open and honest about what we were going through.

Worst thing someone did or said:
I think the hardest thing was when people attempted to identify with my feelings when they had some mild version of infertility or just difficulty getting pregnant. Although I am sure the intention was to connect and support, to me it felt like they were not really listening and left me feeling more alone.

Advice for someone going through a similar experience:
* Know that you are not alone. Many, many couples go through infertility, even though it is not widely discussed.
* Talk about it. Not constantly and not necessarily with everyone, but do not feel like you need to be ashamed or that you need to keep it all bottled up inside.
* Take time to have fun together as a couple, whatever that means for you. Infertility can be incredibly difficult for a relationship. Finding less stressful ways to connect is crucial.

Advice for those surrounding the bereaved:

  * Don't try to offer advice or fix the problem. Just listen.
  * If your friend is going through IVF, support her during her bed rest periods by loaning movies or books, bringing lunch, etc.
  * If you have children (especially an infant), be sensitive to how hard that might be for your friend. Do not exclude or avoid her, but be aware that it might be hard for her and respect her decision if she skips a baby shower or other event.

Still Here

| Virginia Williams |

How do you begin to tell the story of a child who died? I'm still not sure, nearly eleven years on from the stillbirth of my son Ben. He was my second child, come to complete my family: father, mother, daughter, and son—the perfect family of four. He was due January 2, 2004.

The pregnancy was uneventful and so different from my first pregnancy. With my daughter, I'd been constantly, ravenously hungry; with Ben, I felt sick and had no appetite for months. It was so easy the second time. Later, I would look back and regret my confidence, my nonchalance with my body's changes. I didn't worry, like I had the first time, about tracking the baby's development or how much weight I was gaining. I exercised when I could, tried to eat right, and thought, after the first trimester was over, this baby was a sure thing. How could he not be?

On December 29th, I went to my doctor for my forty-week checkup, thinking all was well. After Dr. Tobias tried to find

Ben's heartbeat with two different Doppler machines, I refused to allow myself to believe anything other than, *It will all be okay.*

As I walked across the hall to the ultrasound office, the office receptionist called out, "Have a happy New Year!" All I could think was, *If you only knew.*

Even so, I refused to hold the thought that something was seriously wrong. As I lay on the ultrasound table, I planned what to say to my husband on the phone, how to tell him the baby was coming now, but that it was fine, just fine—trying to talk myself into believing my own thoughts. But when a doctor walked into the room and grasped my hand, then softly asked how I was feeling, I knew it was all over.

This is how one world ends and another one begins.

In the morning, after a night of tears and shock, Ben. At 6:01 a.m., New Year's Eve morning 2003, my beautiful boy arrived, 19.5 inches, 7 lbs., 10 oz., a perfect little boy in every way except one. It was immediately obvious why he had died: his umbilical cord was tied in a tight knot, pulled taut sometime the day before, ending his life instantly.

Nothing prepares you for this. How to get up every day and put one foot in front of the other. How to remember to breathe. How to endure. No one tells you how many tears you will cry. How many dishes you will hurl at the wall in a white-hot fury. How long you will spend trying not to believe what you know is true. He will not breathe, no matter how much you beg, and there is no going back to the place of blissful innocence where you once lived.

There hasn't been a day in all these years that I haven't thought of him, missed him, and loved him. Some people think me odd for missing someone I never really knew. I think them odd for not understanding that Ben is my son and a part of my life and my thoughts every day, just like his living siblings. He may not be here in my arms, but he is here in my heart. I can't forget him any more than I can forget the daughter and son who are able to receive my hugs. I won't ever stop remembering him, talking about him, and loving him. He is still here.

People will tell you that grief is the price you pay for love. Though I wish it wasn't so, I know it to be true. I would never wish Ben had not existed, just to spare me the grief of his loss. He changed us, and though I wish I'd never felt the pain his death brought, I'm so glad I had the time with him that I did. It's a hard-won emotion, this sense of gratitude. There's no simple path to finding it.

Yes, grief and love walk hand in hand. Though the pain has ebbed, I carry Ben—his life and death—within me. I know that while grief changes and lessens with time, love never does.

Best thing someone did or said:
The best thing anyone said to me was, "I don't know what to say because I don't know how you feel. I'm just so sorry." It was a great relief to have someone acknowledge that she didn't know how I felt and not try to make it better or compare losses.

Worst thing someone did or said:
Where to begin? I was told, "Move on," "Let it be a learning and growing experience," "It happened for a reason," "God must've needed another angel," "You'll have another baby," "At least you have your daughter." There were people who wanted me to make it easier for *them*. There were others who refused to acknowledge my son was a real person.

Advice for someone going through a similar experience:
* You don't get over love. You will carry your love for your child for the rest of your life.
* There are no rules for grief, no timeline or future date when it will all be better. Grief takes as long as it takes, and no one can tell you how long that will be.

Advice for those surrounding the bereaved:
* Listen without advising, without judgment, without expectation.

(continued on next page)

(continued from previous page)

* When you don't know what to say, it's all right to say just that, along with a simple, "I'm so sorry."
* Offer specific suggestions: "I can walk your dog on Tuesday." "Want me to pick up the kids up after school on Thursday?" "I'll make you a meal on Saturday." Often it's too hard for the bereaved to ask for help, or even to think of what they might need.

Other Kinds of Loss

Valerie Harper

| Actress |

I'm Valerie Harper, who played the character Rhoda Morgenstern on TV. I was diagnosed in 2013 with leptomeningeal carcinomitosis (lepto, for short), an extremely rare, terminal, incurable cancer located in the lining of my brain, the meninges. It was estimated that I had three months or so to live.

Good Grief! I didn't want to hear that! Neither did my dear family, loved ones, devoted friends, gifted colleagues, fans, pals, good-will wishers, supporters, folks I've brought to laughter or tears, nor the endless number of people I've encountered throughout my long and wonderful life.

Because of the shocking finality of my diagnosis, my poor husband, Tony, too devastated and too infuriated to break the news to me, let our daughter Cristina convey the doctor's prognosis. I remember her lovely green eyes, wide with disbelief, as she asked, "Didn't Dad tell you? Three months, six months at the most, Mom."

At first, Tony refused to accept that I had an "incurable" illness. He always countered, "So far it's incurable, but a cure could be just around the corner." That plus regular exercise, consistent walking, nutritious foods, a conscientious pill regimen, and other beneficial actions, such as listening to Tony, not giving up, and focusing on the moments we were sharing. Enjoying every minute and being eternally grateful for our fabulous partnership in life, business, and love.

Our main focus now is trying to get us back to living as normal a life as possible, with goals, trips, and things of interest to look forward to.

So my advice is to grab "the Tony method" and approach your person facing loss with support that is specific to what they need. And I'm not just referring to a mate. Any age, any relationship, simply be there as BEST FRIEND.

Sightings

| Jane Blanchard |

"Le coeur a ses raisons que la raison ne connaît point."
—Blaise Pascal, *Les Pensées, 1665*

Across the campus walks a woman—young, white, tall,
and slender, very blonde. I glance at her then stare
until attempts at recognition fail, as all
such eager efforts do—here, there, and everywhere.

I cannot stop my eye from turning or my mind
from churning at the prospect of a daughter long
lost found well. When I claim to be at last resigned
to absence, longing means that logic can go wrong.

For years she saw each glass half empty, and with love
I simply said, "Not so, half full," but then one day,
enough being enough, I flipped the glass to prove
my point and watched the water run, her run away.

The same old question begs an easy answer: how
can someone once familiar be a stranger now?

Best thing someone did or said:
"You did your best."

Worst thing someone did or said:
"You didn't do enough."

Advice for someone going through a similar experience:
It's not your fault.

Advice for those looking to provide support to someone in a similar situation:
You have no idea.

Giuliana Rancic

| Actress, Author |

When I was first diagnosed with breast cancer and gearing up for my double mastectomy, a lot of my friends were killing me with kindness and sympathy, which I loved, but made me feel sicker and more helpless.

One of my friends, however, talked to me like a normal person and never let me feel sorry for myself. She just kept telling me that I was stronger than I believed I was, and that I needed to live my life to the maximum and not lie in bed and complain all day. She talked to me like the woman I was before the diagnosis, and never treated me differently. I loved that. She also didn't ask me if she could help. Instead, she would do. For example, she wouldn't ask if I needed groceries or wanted a good book or magazines to help me pass the time. Instead, she surprised me every few days by dropping off a package at my door with the latest celebrity magazines, snacks, and goodies. Knowing that I might be feeling down or tired at that moment and not wanting anyone to see me, she would leave before texting me that there was a bag for me at my door.

Those thoughtful gestures and those real conversations always put a smile on my face and kept me believing that I was just facing a hiccup and that my life would soon get back to normal and that I would be the woman I used to be before I knew it. And guess what? I was!

To Your Courage and to Your Grief

| Stephanie Hoffman |

Dedicated to my son Matthew

Best thing someone did or said:

* Best thing I did for myself: Painting was the way I survived when my son Matthew left home at eighteen to join the US Army as an Infantry soldier. He served in and survived the Iraq war. This is a portrait I painted of him during that time.

* Best thing others did for me: Acknowledged the value of what my son—and so many soldiers—were doing.

Worst thing someone did or said:

"I don't believe in war; is he on a death mission?"

Advice for someone going through a similar experience:

* Confide in someone close to you. I'm also a big fan of therapy.

* Do not isolate yourself, no matter how much you want to (and you will want to). Say yes to invitations.

* Feeling afraid and curling up in a ball will not help your soldier. You, too, have to become a soldier.

Advice for those looking to provide support to someone in a similar situation:

Reach out. Love is behavior. You don't need to fill up the air with talk or try to fix the situation. Sometimes it's enough just to sit with that person and be.

Scott Hamilton

| Olympic Gold Medalist,
TV Figure Skating Commentator |

For too long in my life, I felt I was cursed. It seemed that any time something good happened to me, something devastating would soon follow. At the peak of my professional career, for instance, I was diagnosed with testicular cancer. Cancer was the disease that took the center of my universe—my mother—from me.

It was while attending a cancer survivor celebration that I heard a teenage girl, who lost her leg to cancer, say, "The worst thing that happened to me was cancer. But I'm here to say, the best thing that happened to me was cancer." Hearing those words captured everything I was missing. It was like the skies parted and the angels sang, because I realized that soon after my diagnosis of cancer, something inside me awakened that allowed me to know who I was and what I was capable of doing. The curse of cancer revealed the most powerful aspect of my character.

Lost and Found

| Sue Carloni |

It was before I even started using a cane that it happened. As I walked past a male coworker's desk one day, he said, "Hey, what happened to your wiggle?"

"What do you mean?" I asked.

"It's gone."

"It's not there at all?" I asked in a panic.

He shook his head.

"Watch me again," I said. I walked away, trying hard not to limp. Then I turned around and walked toward him, hopeful he was mistaken. "Well?"

"It's gone, all right."

This time I walked away self-consciously. It's not that I'd ever deliberately wiggled my hips. It just came naturally. But by losing that aspect of my appearance, I suddenly felt different.

I had lost a part of my "old self." A part that had made me a woman. A woman whose wiggle made her feel attractive and feminine. A woman who didn't mind catching men's attention.

Now that my wiggle was gone, I felt plain and unattractive. I wondered if the way I walked looked like a man's stride instead of a woman's sashay. My self-esteem slipped away, along with my smile.

I didn't feel like wearing pretty dresses to work anymore and instead wore slacks and blue jeans. Why bother trying to look like a woman if I couldn't walk like one?

I felt that way for months until one day another male coworker asked what had happened to my smile.

"What do you mean?" I asked

"You hardly ever smile anymore," he said. "And you have such a pretty smile."

I offered a fake grin and limped away. When I sat down at my desk, I recalled other people telling me over the years what a nice smile I had and how I always looked happy and bubbly.

I realized I had allowed a positive aspect of myself to disappear. An aspect I could have kept, despite the encroachments of multiple sclerosis. An aspect over which I did have control.

I resumed wearing dresses to the office and once again was my usual bubbly self. Although I couldn't wiggle when I walked, I could still wear pretty dresses and flash a genuine smile.

I still miss my wiggle occasionally. But even when I walk with my cane, I feel every bit a feminine woman, and I'm not afraid to smile about it.

Dedicated to my husband, Kurt (1953–2015)

Best thing someone did or said:
A co-worker told me I have always had a pretty smile and bubbly personality, which lifted my spirits.

Worst thing someone did or said:
A friend told me I should try to walk without a cane for as long as I could so that I would look "normal."

Advice for someone going through a similar experience:
* The person inside you is what's important; not your physical appearance.
* Don't listen to what others say.
* Accept your circumstances; stay positive.

Advice for those looking to provide support to someone in a similar situation:
* Accept the individual as they are when their physical appearance changes.
* Treat the person the same way you always have.
* Offer compliments.

Olivia Newton-John

| Actress, Singer |

My most memorable moment was after I told my Buddhist friend,
Jim Chuda, and his wife, Nancy, of my breast cancer diagnosis in
1992. Jim said to me, "Congratulations—for now you will grow."

It stuck with me even though in that moment I didn't quite
understand it. It was one of the most poignant and confirming
things said to me at that time—that he believed in me to grow
and go forward. That has been absolutely my experience.

Forgetful

| Andrea Stewart |

I forgot . . . that I was happy;
I went to work and was genuinely able to smile.

I forgot that I had friends;
Not in my regular life, cause I was a loner, but in my work life.

I'm generally always alone,
Surrounded by others and a part of nothing,
But not at work, until now . . .

I forgot . . . how much I enjoyed working hard;
Doing my job, making a good impression.

I forgot . . . you can't find this everywhere;
I got stupid for all the wrong reasons and made a move
that destroyed it all.

I forgot how much this place has changed me into a version I didn't know I could be.

Was it real? Is she really me?

I remember now, but it's too late.

Never will I ever let myself feel this way again.
I can never again forget.

Best thing someone did or said:
They got me out of the house to take my mind off everything.

Worst thing someone did or said:
"I kind of resent you for putting everything on me."

Advice for someone going through a similar experience:
- Get out of your head by getting out of the house. Go see a movie, go to the beach, hang out with friends. Don't lock yourself away while you're in a sour mood. It only makes it worse.
- Don't try moving ahead until you've forgiven yourself. If you try moving on too soon, your horrible mood will leak into your attempts at fixing your situation.

Advice for those looking to provide support to someone in a similar situation:
- Be supportive, but not overbearing.
- Give them their space by letting them come to you with their issues.

Mental Health

| Janne Karlsson |

MENTAL HEALTH

I'll show you
mental health

I'll show you how to
cover your scars

to kiss the vacuum
of silence

to dance like a lunatic
in a dead end universe

mental health
I'll show you mental health.

JANNE
KARLSSON '14

Best thing someone did or said:
Even though I'm a not a religious person, I found the Serenity Prayer helpful. Accept the things I cannot change . . .

Worst thing someone did or said:
"You don't look very depressed to me." "I don't believe there's anything wrong, too." (My doctor)

Advice for someone going through a similar experience:
* Take a deep breath and analyze the problem. Is this even a problem? Is this just a bad feeling you can control?
* If it's a feeling you can control, get out in the open air and exercise, take a walk, lift some weights.
* If not, seek professional psychiatric help.

Advice for those looking to provide support to someone in a similar situation:
Actually, the suggestions above apply just as well here.

Wild Stallion

| Isabella Schwinn |

The freezing wind was blowing that night as my boyfriend and I walked by Ocean Beach. We had just been out for dinner at the first place we ever ate as a couple. It wasn't just a restaurant; it was *our* restaurant. A year later, here we were, as giggly as the day we first began. He was jumping on sand dunes and posing for ridiculous pictures. I held his hand and we sat down on a bench to enjoy the sunset. I loved the way he laughed at himself, the way his nose sat so crookedly on his face. I loved to touch his beardy chin and snuggle into his chest. I loved his imagination, his outlook on life, and his unbridled creativity. He was a wild stallion, ready to run free.

The cold wind whistled through the hoods of our jackets, so we decided to keep walking. He was leading us in a really strange direction, toward the back streets behind the beach.

"It's too cold for this to be fun." I shivered. "I think we should go to my house and make a fire."

He didn't reply. His brow was furrowed, and he just kept walking.

"Let's go to my house and make a fire," I repeated.

Again, he ignored my request. We started to cross the street.

"Why don't you want to come over to my house?" I said.

"Because I don't want to date you anymore," he replied.

I was standing in the middle of the road.

"Are you serious?" I responded.

"Let's get off the road," he said.

"You're the one who told me this while I was crossing the street!" I yelled.

"Look, it's really hard for me to tell you this . . ." He trailed off.

My heart throbbed in my chest, my eyes wide with disbelief. "I need to be alone right now," I said.

"Do you *want* me to go away?" he asked.

I had never wanted him to leave my side. "Yes," I said, stunned.

"Call me when you get home," he stammered. Then he turned and walked away.

I stood on that street corner for a minute, watching him leave my life. I remember that he was wearing a shirt that he brought out only for special dinners with me. That was *our* shirt. I remember he had bought a new hat online that day while we were talking on the phone—choosing it together. That was *our* hat. I remember watching his silhouette grow small until he turned a corner and was gone. That was the last moment I saw him, the last moment I shared physical space with the only man I have ever truly loved.

Truth be told, he was never really mine. Our restaurant, our shirt, our hat, our time together were all borrowed. There are moments I find myself wishing I could rewind time. Prepare myself. Maybe I could have broken up with him first? Maybe if I hadn't gone to the beach with him that night we would still be together? My memory can (and will) sugarcoat his actions and cloud the red flags. I can choose to see this as a rejection—or as a gift to my future self. Maybe it was the golden ticket I needed to become the woman I am supposed to be?

I don't believe that we get everything we want in this life. I also don't believe that we truly own anything that we have. I don't believe that there is one, single, solitary man out there for me—or that I will miss the opportunity for love and marriage if I fail to meet that "one." My heart has broken, and it will break again. But I will still put one foot in front of the other. I acknowledge the daily pain I feel in other people's happiness, and the holes in my own. I have chosen to feel the emotions that break within me. I have accessed stores of strength. Every day gets easier, and I know that in the end I am going to be just fine.

Best thing someone did or said:
"An answered prayer doesn't always feel good."

Worst thing someone did or said:
"I knew he was a jerk."

Advice for someone going through a similar experience:
Feel what needs to be felt, and then move on. Make an active choice to steer your life toward the next opportunity. Wallowing in the past won't propel you in the direction you were born to go.

Advice for those looking to provide support to someone in a similar situation:
Allow a month where the person in the breakup can freely talk about what's going on. After a month, if it seems the person isn't able to move forward, gently suggest that they seek professional help.

Pitching Through the Pain

| Brad F. |

My whole life I dreamed of playing professional baseball. From the time I could walk, my dad had me outside in the backyard practicing . . . every day . . . every night. In my mind, there was no question *if* I would make it to the majors; the only question was *when*.

After playing competitively through primary and secondary school, I was recruited by a university and offered a full, duel academic and athletic scholarship. My dream was becoming a reality. By sophomore year, I was well on my way to breaking the school record for the most wins by a pitcher.

All of that came to a screeching halt my junior year when I tore my rotator cuff. Initially, I didn't realize that my physical torment was anything more than a pulled muscle, so I played through the pain—for an entire season. By the end of the year I could barely lift my arm. When the doctor delivered the diagnosis, he said I had two options: (1) undergo surgery, red shirt my senior year, and hope that the rehab worked well enough for me to compete the following year; or (2) pitch through the pain and regard my senior year as the end of my baseball career.

Mine was a grief that perhaps only another athlete could understand. I felt like my life, my hopes, and my dreams had all been compromised.

At a crossroads, I turned my attention in a different direction to reach my decision. At the time, I was three years into a relationship with a woman whom I knew I wanted to marry. Instead of asking, "What's best for me?" I asked myself, "What's best for us as a couple?" With that, the answer became clear.

I played my senior year. Though I didn't break the school record or get drafted, I ended up getting so much more. I've since found a career that I love and, in case you were wondering (c'mon, you know you were), I married my girlfriend. My lifelong hopes and dreams became new hopes and dreams. In the end, everything has worked out better than I could have imagined.

For my wife, Julia

Best thing someone did or said:
My coach told me that I reignited his passion for coaching because of my determination to pitch through the pain.

Worst thing someone did or said:
Things like "Well, at least you had a good run!" and "Come on, you didn't really think you'd go pro, did you?" At such moments, all I wanted was to be alone. I didn't want opinions about why I did or didn't make the right decision. I just wanted time to grieve my old dreams, and make room for my new ones.

Advice for someone going through a similar experience:
Everything happens for a reason. Always learn from your experiences.

Advice for those looking to provide support to someone in a similar situation:
Instead of telling the person what you *think* they want to hear, ask them how they want to be treated. If they want support, be there.

My Morning Delight

| Sheree K. Nielsen |

In the stillness of the early morning, the owl is who-ing and the morning birds are chirping softly. Daylight peeks through the blinds, casting tiny sunbeams on the carpet. Comfortably snuggled beneath cotton sheets, my husband and I enjoy the cool breeze that envelops the room as the ceiling fan moves air downward. Eyes still closed, I feel four small paws walking on me, followed by a gentle nudge on my forearm.

Awaking, I smile at my little friend. With every purr, I feel the beating of his heart. With every look, I see the love in his eyes. With every touch, I sense the wisdom and the gentleness in his feline soul.

"I love you, Scooby."

My husband, still in dreamland, answers, "I love you."

Only Scooby knows the truth.

*In memory of Scooby, who entered this world
with a roar and left with a quiet whisper
(October 13, 1996—February 12, 2011)*

Best thing someone did or said:
  ** My friends said to me, "You'll get to see Scooby again in heaven. He's no longer in pain. He's running on Rainbow Ridge, carefree with all the other animals."
  * My father-in-law, Pat Nielsen, sent me a card and a sweet poem about where pets go when they pass from this life. How, when a beloved pet reaches Rainbow Ridge, there's no more suffering—only meadows of green—where they can run and play. Animals are happy and waiting for their owners to come one day so they can be together forever.

Worst thing someone did or said:
I try not to dwell on the negative; so if there was anything negative said or done, I blocked it out.

Advice for someone going through a similar experience:
Everyone grieves differently. Some people take longer to get over a pet. Do what your heart tells you. If you think it's time to get another pet, then do so. There are so many cats and dogs in the world that need love.

Advice for those surrounding the bereaved:
  * Be understanding.
  * Be compassionate.
  * Listen.

My Darling Companion

| Gerri Leen |

The patter of little feet is stilled
I've cleaned up the toys
Donated favorite food
It will help others
The house resounds with the lack of him
Echoing silence, emptiness in every room
A hole in my heart in his shape
With his eyes
Those bright, bright eyes
So wise for his years
He was a gift
Even if I only had him for five years
He kept me sane
He kept me warm inside
when life blew frigid winds
Cuddling him next to me
was the only thing that calmed
He never left me
Others did, others always did

He stayed; he was mine
I was his
He shared my life with me
So what if he was a cat?
"Just a cat," I heard at work
"So much drama for just a cat"
Because I took the day off
I had to say good-bye
Had it been my child
One day would seem callously short
But this earns a "Sheesh"
Maybe "Get a grip"
Never to my face, but I hear them
I pity them when I'm not mired in hurt
When I can see beyond my pain
They've never loved an animal
Or they'd realize
Loss is loss
Companions come in all species

Dedicated to Kilana

Best thing someone did or said:
My friends let me grieve and they didn't judge when I got new cats relatively soon after losing my girl. I think acceptance is the greatest gift.

Worst thing someone did or said:
Fortunately, when I lost my cat I was working with fellow pet lovers, so hugs, cards, and understanding were abundant. I have a friend who was not so lucky. When she called in to say that she wouldn't be coming to the office the day after putting her animal down, she was told, "It's just a cat."

Advice for someone going through a similar experience:
* Grieve your loss in a way that feels right for you. Don't worry if it's not how others would handle a similar experience.
* Your grief is real. Don't pay attention to people who try to diminish your sense of loss.

Advice for those surrounding the bereaved:
* Be accepting and don't judge. Everyone mourns in their own way and at their own pace.
* After the loss of a pet, don't try to push a replacement on the grieving individual before they are ready.
* Be sure you're not trying to accelerate the grieving individual's healing process to make yourself more comfortable.

Loss and Time

Montel Williams

| Actor, Author, TV Host |

The best advice anyone has ever given me in a time of personal loss was offered after my grandmother passed away. Over the years, I have shared it with others. It's especially poignant when people are reflecting during the first few days of grieving the loss of a loved one, family member or friend.

A Native American proverb, circa 600 A.D., the saying goes like this: "When you are born you cry and the world rejoices. You should live your life so that when you die the world can cry and you can rejoice."

As you experience the feelings of your loss and remember the person you are grieving, there should be solace in knowing that they lived their life in such a way that you feel they deserve your tears, but also remember that they wouldn't want you to wallow in your tears.

Three Little Words

| Kaye Ambrose |

Are you okay? That is the question I am asked most often since my mother died. It is a simple question. Just three little words. Yet answering that question is so difficult.

Yes, I am okay. Thank you for asking!

This is my go-to answer. My polite answer. It is the answer for people who ask out of obligation or general awkwardness. It is the answer I know, rationally, I should give. I have my health, a job I love, and obviously my life didn't end because my mother's did. I know, rationally, my mother is finally free of pain. That her poor, disease-ravaged body is finally at rest. I am slowly starting to accept her passing. I am slowly starting to accept that I will, indeed, be okay. Except . . .

No, I am not okay!

Are you kidding me? My mother is dead! Of course I am not okay! The irrational side of me feels like screaming it at everyone who asks. It is a ridiculous question. She was sick for so long, and I took care of her alone. Even now, her sleep schedule is mine, waking in the middle of the night according to when she needed to go to the bathroom or just wanted to talk.

How could I possibly be okay when the only parent I have ever known is suddenly gone? The woman who could look at me and know before my second foot came through the door if I was hurting, angry, or ill. I will never again see her smile light up her eyes or feel her pat my hand because one of us is afraid and too stubborn to admit it.

I feel like an orphan. Silly, I know, because I am an adult. Yet, it is true. I feel like I am wandering aimlessly, searching for a vital piece of myself. I know what it is. I know that it is gone forever. I feel the burning, aching void. Except . . .

Another day has passed, and while I miss her terribly, the burning is a little less intense, the aching a little less distracting.

I don't know how I am doing, but . . .

Today I feel calmer. I am not quite so lost. I notice that I am crying a little less and laughing a little more at my memories. My sadness, still with me all the time, doesn't consume me anymore. How am I? I am doing better. For now, better is all I can ask.

In memory of my mother, who passed away in 2014

Best thing someone did or said:
My best friend has two daughters, ages ten and three. They never said anything to me about my mother dying or asked why I was so upset. They just followed me around, and when I sat down, they snuggled up next to me and whispered, "We don't want anything; we just want to be close to you."

Worst thing someone did or said:
Asking me, ten minutes after I received the news that she was gone, if my mother had left me anything good in her will then telling me that it was good she died because now I was free to live my own life.

Advice for someone going through a similar experience:
* Surround yourself with people who bring you comfort.
* Don't get sucked into useless arguments.
* If you need to be alone to grieve, then do it. Trying to hold your grief inside will only make it worse.

Advice for those surrounding the bereaved:
* If you have no idea what to say, then don't say anything. Give them a hug, hold their hand, or sit beside them until they are ready to talk.
* Don't say, "Call me if you need anything" if you don't mean it.
* Don't act like they should get over the death after a couple of days. They are dealing with death, not a head cold.

Gone

| Rosanne Trost |

My first husband died too young. He was 37.
Our daughters were 5 and 7 years old.
His parents lived until their 90s.

Although, for four months, I knew he was dying,
the death was a shock.
A relief that his pain and suffering had come to an end.
Still the shock. A closing door, now slammed shut.

My own pain and suffering continued, but on a new path.
I was unprepared for these new circumstances.
Always tired. So much responsibility.
Too many lonely decisions.
Enduring all the important occasions that first year.
Somehow, they were easier than the ordinary days.
But nothing was ordinary anymore.

One year later, the pain seemed even more pronounced.
A gaping hole. When will the grieving stop? I missed him.

The grief books had encouraged me to just get through that first year.

What went wrong? I had read and clung to those books.

Two steps forward.

Never knowing how many backward steps.

The forward steps did continue and increase.

"God looks out for widows and orphans."

Perhaps, that is true. A hymn,

"Blessed are you who weep and mourn, for someday you shall laugh."

I prayed that someday I would laugh.

There were many stumbles, and some big falls, along the way.

Somehow, we were protected.

All these years later, I see through the long ago pain.

The many good things that have come my way.

Inner strength. Sense of accomplishment. Laughing at outrageous fears.

Their dad's birthday, his 74th, was in May.

He has now been gone for as many years as he lived.

Dedicated to my daughters, Laura and Jane

Best thing someone did or said:
"The spirit of your husband is with you and your children."
"Talk to him about your fears."

Worst thing someone did or said:
"You are young. You will get married again."

Advice for someone going through a similar experience:
* Healing takes time. Do not try to rush it.
* Holidays may be easier to bear than ordinary days.
* Ask friends for their help. They want to be there for you.

Advice for those surrounding the bereaved:
* Do not avoid talking about the death. Listen, even though it may be hard.

Lauren

| Elizabeth Barker |

Although your time with us was just three short years, you taught us a lifetime of lessons and gifted us with unforgettable memories.

You taught us *Courage* as we watched you fight for your life at birth, determined to triumph over your complex health issues.

You taught us *Happiness & Joy* as your health improved and, despite your difficult start, your engaging personality—enthusiastic, fun loving, and always so entertaining—emerged.

You taught us *True & Unconditional Love* as we ricocheted between deep worry and unfettered joy.

You taught us *Hope* as we faced each new health challenge. Because of you, we learned to let optimism, not pessimism, guide; to believe in the power within to overcome and succeed; to experience both the good and the bad in people and in situations; to focus on the positive and shun negative energy.

In memory of Lauren Elizabeth Barker

Best thing someone did or said:

* I particularly appreciated when people would recall a happy event that they had shared with us and our precious daughter. Sure, I might get teary eyed, maybe even cry, but simultaneously I was very pleased and grateful that someone cared enough to dig deep and share a special memory about my daughter.

* The most touching moment: A good friend, who also has a special needs child, called me on my first Christmas Day without Lauren to say that she understood how difficult this first big holiday without my daughter was for me. Her call came months after Lauren had passed, and at a time when I am sure my friend was busy with her own holiday celebration. I will never forget her thoughtfulness in taking the time to reach out and comfort me.

Worst thing someone did or said:

Maybe it was because Lauren had Down syndrome, but too often well-meaning people spouted the trite phrase, "She's in a better place now." I know this expression is often used when the deceased was elderly or sickly and is meant to provide solace, but this phrase just reeks of "I don't know what to say" or "I don't care enough to say something personal or meaningful to comfort you."

(continued on next page)

(continued from previous page)

Advice for someone going through a similar experience:

 * Feel free to share your memories. I love reminiscing about my daughter with people who knew her and our family. Too many people fear that they are going to upset you by talking about your deceased loved one. Uncomfortable with your emotions and your tears, they shy away. This is so wrong. It is upsetting if the birthday of the deceased passes and no one mentions her name. It is upsetting if no one is willing to reminisce fondly about your loved one at special family events or on special days.

 * To honor what would have been my daughter's twenty-fifth birthday, I threw a party to benefit the charity that helped her and us during her short life. The party was a huge success financially, but more importantly it was an emotional high for me that filled me with love and positive energy. I knew that people were there to support me in honoring the memory of my daughter and to pay it forward to other families like ours who needed this organization's support and services. That was such a win-win day.

Advice for those surrounding the bereaved:

 * If you duck the bereaved or avoid talking to them about those who have passed, it conveys that you don't care enough to take the time to say or do something meaning-

ful. It makes no sense to shove their loss under the carpet and to try to forget about what happened; nor does it make sense to think that by mentioning the deceased you are re-opening an emotional wound. Instead, take the time to be sincere and thoughtful. Think what you would want if you were in the grieving person's shoes.

* The bereaved appreciate it when people do special things to honor the memory of their loved one. Think about making a donation to a charity that is meaningful to the bereaved in memory of their loved one, especially on a holiday or on the birthday or date of death of the deceased.

Speaking of Grief

| Joanna Pocock |

"No one ever told me that grief felt so like fear."
—C. S. Lewis, *A Grief Observed*

This sentence, better than any other, captures a painful truth about grief: nothing prepares you for it.

Almost nine years ago, my sister Mary died in Toronto, at the age of fifty-two. For many days after the news of her death reached me in London, I lay in bed unable to do anything but cry. One of the most terrible things about grief is that it fades with time, no matter how hard we hold onto it. And we do hold onto it. Letting go of our grief is like saying "yes" to the death of the person we are mourning. By holding onto it, we think we are holding onto the person we love. But how wrong we are.

Towards the end of his essay, Lewis does come to a sort of acceptance of his wife's death when he says, "I will turn to her as often as possible in gladness. I will even salute her with a laugh. The less I mourn her the nearer I seem to her." Over the years, I have come to a similar place. I can smile when I think of my sister, and I can talk about her without crying. Yet strangely I feel as close to her as I did in the early stages of mourning.

This paradigm shift towards acceptance happens despite us. It reminds that grieving is a process, not a fixed state.

At Mary's funeral, the thought I couldn't shake was: "I don't know how to do this. I need Mary to tell me how." She had always been there to advise me about every aspect of life. After she was gone, I had to think, "What would Mary do?" And, oddly, it sort of worked. Faced with an invitation to a party, for instance, I would ask myself, "Would Mary want me to go?" Invariably, she would.

I so remember, after my sister's death, the sense that the world as I knew it was no longer recognizable. Words I had been using all my life felt empty and meaningless. My sister was appearing to me at night and giving me instructions. She was so like herself in my dreams that when I awoke I could barely believe she was no longer alive. I could not understand her presence in my life, the fact that she was so much there and yet so absolutely not there.

It has taken me these nine years to process my loss and to see it as something worth writing about. I have come to realize that grief is both universal and terribly specific. Talking about death and loss should be part of life. I want to pass on a vocabulary of grief to my daughter. Some day she will no doubt find herself mourning the death of someone she loves. Some day she may find solace in C. S. Lewis or perhaps in something yet to be written. I hope she can find the words and use them to navigate her way through the terror, the confusion, the sense of utter loss and desperation that comes from losing someone who has in essence become part of oneself. I don't want her to say, "No one ever told me grief felt so like fear." I want her to *know* it feels like fear and so many other things. Unnamed things. Unwritten things. Things that will be specific to her and yet linked to every person who has loved someone and watched them die.

In memory of Mary Pocock

Best thing someone did or said:
Friends who listened, rather than those who wanted to "fix" the situation, were invaluable.

Worst thing someone did or said:
"Why are you so moody?"

Advice for someone going through a similar experience:
Allow the feelings to pass through you, and feel them as they do. Fighting them only makes it worse. Talking therapy is invaluable, especially from a dedicated grief counselor.

Advice for those surrounding the bereaved:

 * Don't try to stop the mourning. Allow the person to feel what they are feeling and to manifest these feelings in whatever way the griever needs to.
 * Avoid judging and give the griever space. Be there if they need you, but try not to offer unwanted advice.

Petals

| Elizabeth Charles |

Meeting you for the first time —
your words to me
innocuous but memorable,
eight simple words
I can still recall
half my lifetime later.

Our first kiss —
a potent mix of promise, of desire,
and of wishes not previously recognized
come true.

Time blurs in
smiles and whispers,
music videos and scooter rides.
Late night confidences and
lazy morning kisses.

All of it —
so close and yet so long ago.

I emerge from my
trip down the past
breathless;
longing for what
has been taken away,
but marveling at what remains:
Delicate petals of memory
to peel away
for the rest of my life.

Best thing someone did or said:
My mom and I had never said, "I love you" to each other. During the grieving period, she was there for me every day. Following a particularly emotional phone call, I said to her, "Thank you for taking such good care of me. I love you." She responded, "I love you, too." Ever since then, she and I have been the best of friends.

Worst thing someone did or said:
I felt abandoned by one particular friend. I didn't feel he was available for me in the months that followed my loss. Even if he had just sent a quick email every couple of days saying he was busy but thinking about me, that would have helped.

Advice for someone going through a similar experience:
You may feel the urge to distract yourself (e.g., by working all the time, over-scheduling yourself, etc.) so you don't have to experience the pain of grief. But the pain won't kill you, as much as it may seem that way. Try not to avoid your grief. Acknowledge it.

Advice for those surrounding the bereaved:
Remind the person that it hurts because they loved so much. This is something to be proud of.

Regrowing the Forest

| Christine Emmert |

The fire has downed all that was once tall and healthy,
and spread the world flat again.
We look upon the ashes.
We smell the destruction even after,
as we sensed it even during.
What we loved and lived in
is that which we grew together—
one landscape to contain us both—
for which you provided
the sun and moon and careful rains
of nourishment.
Now we must find the seeds again
and start the growing
of a new existence
where memories blend with sprouted seedlings
of hope.
We must start again to be aware
of what makes us happy.

We look to future woodlands
inspired by past plantings of joy
and even sorrow.
You are gone,
but you are here
as new life disguised.

In memory of my son, Jason

Best thing someone did or said:
"Everyone's time comes to an end . . . some have a long life while still very young."

Worst thing someone did or said:
"God needed an angel."

Advice for someone going through a similar experience:
We plan a life when we join someone in love. The loss of that life takes away a geography from us. It's okay to be angry and to weep. Don't be bitter. Bitterness shuts you down. Anger and grief move you on.

Advice for those surrounding the bereaved:
Let people talk about their grief. Don't try to make them quiet. They need the words to understand it, even if those words make you uncomfortable.

Handprints, Footprints, Heart-prints

| Lori Miroslaw |

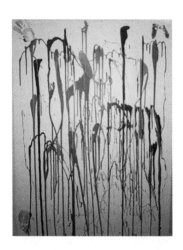

After my sister learned that her newborn daughter had an undeveloped heart chamber that would make for a life numbered in days, not years, she asked our brother and me to be little Brooke's godparents. I felt very special and blessed to hold my niece as she was baptized right there in the hospital. It also felt special that my sister brought Brooke to the workouts that I structured for my sister to help her endure the pain that attended knowing Brooke's destiny. For four months, I got to enjoy Brooke's presence while I worked with my sister. As emotional as those months were, it made me proud that I was Brooke's godmother and was able to be a part of her short life.

Best thing someone did or said:
We had many people show up and just sit with us. Their presence was comforting.

Worst thing someone did or said:
At least she passed in her father's arms at home.

Advice for someone going through a similar experience:

* When you know someone's time is short, find ways to store your memories. Write a poem or story about your loved one. Keep a journal. Take photos.
* Be creative. In my case, my sister's other daughter was having a tough time accepting Brooke's fate. So, for my niece's fourth birthday party, we came up with an activity that we hoped would forever entwine her life with that of her baby sister's. We set a large canvas on the floor, explained we were going to make a painting in honor of Brooke, and then invited all the young guests to contribute. As Brooke looked on, the kids dripped paint on the canvas. As a final touch, we put Brooke's footprint in the lower left lower corner of the canvas, and my older niece's handprint in an upper left corner. Brooke died not long after. Years later, the painting still hangs in my sister's home.
* Surround yourself with family and good friends who are compassionate and understand the difficulty associated

(continued on next page)

(continued from previous page)

with losing a loved one. When I lost my dad last year, my family found solace in getting through the hard times together.

* Remember time is always a great healer. Memories last forever . . .

Advice for those surrounding the bereaved:

Appreciate what you have and those you love.

Takeaways

What you might say
or write . . .

1. I am so sorry for your loss.
2. I am truly sorry.
3. We send our condolences.
4. I wish I had helpful words, but just know that I care. I am here.
5. I could not possibly know how you are feeling, but I will always be here for you.
6. (Name) is in my thoughts and prayers.
7. My favorite memory of (Name) is . . .
8. I am always a phone call away, but I will be calling and checking on you.
9. I am here for you.
10. I am usually up early or late; don't hesitate to call if you need anything.
11. I am carrying you in my thoughts and in my heart.
12. My thoughts and prayers are with you.
13. I am thinking of you, I am so sorry.
14. (Name) was such a (wonderful/special/loving/caring/larger than life/amazing) person.

15. I would love to hear stories about (Name) when you are ready.

16. I love you and I am here for you.

17. Our hearts are with you.

18. I am so sorry you are suffering.

19. Remember we love and care about you.

20. I care about you.

21. I pray for you every day.

22. Sending you thoughts of comfort.

23. You are so very important to me.

24. I am so deeply sorry to hear about your loss.

25. With loving memories of . . .

26. (Name) will remain in our hearts and minds forever.

27. We pray God holds you during this time.

28. May you find comfort in the outpouring of love that surrounds you.

29. Sending you thoughts of love and strength.

30. We send our love and condolences.

What you generally should avoid . . .

Remember that, in many kinds of loss, that person is forever changed and no loss is the exact same as another.

1. At least they lived to an old age.
2. They are in a better place.
3. They brought this on themselves.
4. There is a reason for everything.
5. It's been awhile, are you over the sadness?
6. Are you feeling better yet?
7. I know how you feel.
8. They were such a good person God wanted them.
9. I had a similar situation . . .
10. My friend had the same . . .
11. (Name) did what they came here to do and it was their time to go.
12. You need to be strong for your (family/children/parents).
13. At least there is no more suffering.
14. They are at peace now.
15. At least they passed before it got worse.

16. Just think of all the blessings you still have in your life.

17. We know (Name) would not want you to be sad.

18. At least you have so many amazing memories.

19. I can't imagine how horrible this is for you right now.

20. I understand how you feel.

21. Do not try to "fix it' with words. This is something that you cannot fix.

22. At least they are with (Jesus/God/Heaven/Angels.)

23. Call me when you feel like it.

24. If you want me to do something, call me.

25. They would have wanted it this way.

26. Now you will start a new chapter in your life and move forward.

27. I don't know what I would do if my . . . died.

28. At least you got the chance to say good-bye.

29. I know you will feel better soon.

30. You are doing so much better than I thought.

31. Just give it time.

32. You are strong enough to get through this.

33. Try not to think about it.

34. Let's go to the movies so you can forget about it all.

35. This will make you stronger.

36. This is a blessing in disguise.

37. Now you have your own angel in heaven.

38. God only gives you what you can handle.

39. Remember this is not about you. Do not try to bring in your own life stories and experiences during this time.

40. Do not try to put your religious views on someone to try to make them feel better.

Loss of a Child

41. You can have another child still.

42. At least you have other children.

43. Now you have your own special angel in heaven.

Military

44. It is an honor that they died defending our country.

45. They probably didn't even realize what hit them.

46. At least it was fast.

What you might do…

1. Drop off healthy meals.
2. Give a hug instead of saying something.
3. When tragedy strikes, help the person to contact groups of people. It is too much for the person going through loss to repeat the stories and questions over and over.
4. Sit silently and just be with the person.
5. Leave a card saying you are thinking about them in their mailbox.
6. Share a story, memory, or picture of the person.
7. Everyone shows up in the beginning, continue to show up over time and check in.
8. Be there. Attend the funeral. Go to the house. When they are ready, be with them somewhere else, giving them the space to talk or simply to be with you in quiet.
9. Listen without comment or judgment.
10. Offer to do something specific:
    a. I will pick the kids up next week.
    b. Next Wednesday, I will be dropping off dinner.
11. People tend to get uncomfortable and avoid mourners. If appropriate when you see them, give them a hug, hold their hand, or put your arm around them.
12. Send a note, email, or text.

13. Organize some friends with a schedule of tasks and errands for their support.
14. Gather friends and family to plant a memorial garden.
15. Remember important dates and support the person though the years.
16. Offer to go with them to visit the gravesite.
17. If there is a financial burden, help set up a funding page or a way for people to contribute and help.
18. Remember you are not being asked to make the person feel better; you are just there to support them and offer companionship during a difficult time.
19. Use all the resources available to you. Look on websites such as Pinterest for a variety of ideas for thoughtful and helpful sympathy gifts.
20. Donate to a charity in the name of the deceased.
21. If they need professional emotional support, help them get pointed in the right direction.
22. Offer to take them out for a drive or to come over for coffee.
23. Do not try to fix it. It cannot be changed but you can be there with them.
24. Protect your loved one from the masses. All the well wishers could become overwhelming. Offer to help them manage all the incoming support.

Epilogue: One for the Road

When we started putting this book together I never imagined myself writing a piece that would be a part of it. I saw our job as more of aggregators and not contributors.

The last few months have changed my opinion.

You see I am a very private person, I do not wear my health on my sleeve. When I went through the experiences of breast cancer I sent an email to friends and people from work explaining my situation thoroughly. I requested they ask any questions right away and not months later. After that, I wanted to go back to living my life without making that a defining property.

Fast forward seven years and forty years of hair chemicals, yes I have "challenged hair," and I find myself in a new situation. A few months ago, I found out I had a tumor in my bladder (there lies the possible connection to hair chemicals,) one that is independent of anything I had in the past. One that is pretty unusual. I guess lightning can strike with "unusual" more than once in a lifetime. I have been told, as I was before, that I will be just fine after the proper treatment. The treatment, however, is quite a long path.

My point is, we all have challenges in life. Ones that are put in front of us and leave us with lessons about our own strength and courage. I believe we have a choice of how to live with these challenges.

This time, with this new diagnosis, I again chose to keep my situation quiet, except for family, until this minute. I ordered myself a necklace, on the front it says "One Tough Bitch," inside is a picture/engraving of my family. When I feel tired, down, or concerned, I reach for my necklace knowing I can drop into a part of myself, dig in my heels, and stand back up with a smile.

This situation, after putting it in this book is no longer a secret, but again I choose not to make it an important chapter in my life.

This time I thought, why not use this experience and offer a different perspective to the book. One where I answer our four questions before people respond, rather than reflect on past experiences.

So here I go:

What is the best thing I hope someone WILL say to me?
I am glad to know you are going to be just fine.

What is the thing I hope someone WON'T say to me?
You should have told me. I know someone who had the same thing..... I am so sorry, then shooting me a "pity" stare.

What advice do I have for others walking a similar path/and for those that surround them?
I like to buy something that can be a visual strength when my mind gets the better of me. Something I can hold on to, to recharge my battery when I feel a little off.

Make sure to do what YOU want and not what others around you want you to do.

Sometimes in life, it helps when you can front-load what you actually want people to say or not say. I understand this is very different when it comes to the loss of a loved one, and any other type of sudden tragedy.

Some people want a lot of support. Some people need support because their strength is zapped from treatments. Some people want to go on walks or do something to raise awareness for their condition. I believe many of these things are very common and helpful.

Then there are oddballs like me who want to just move on and be treated exactly how you treated me before you knew this information.

Each of us is different. The loss is a part of who we become, but perhaps not how we want to be viewed.

This book came at just the right time. I didn't need to send the email this time, I could just write it here.

—Shelly

Acknowledgments

We extend our most sincere gratitude to all those who helped make this collection possible. First and foremost, a very special thank you to all the contributors who were willing to share their stories with us; you are the heart of this collection. Each and every one of you has made a difference in our lives. It was truly our pleasure to have the opportunity to share in your work and experience.

We would also like to thank our co-workers and families for accommodating all of the meetings, late nights, and endless questions. Your support and encouragement was key to making this a success.

To Jill Smolowe, our voice of reason, there aren't enough expressions of gratitude in the world to convey how much we appreciate all you have done for us. You pulled us forward at a time when a sense of direction was crucial. You were always available without hesitation, and we couldn't have asked for anyone better. You're just as much a part of this as we are and we are honored to have worked by your side.

Lastly, to Scot Fisher and Nora Spillane, our other halves who have kept us grounded with unwavering love and support, you both are at the center of all we do, thank you.

About the Authors

Jennifer Jones

Jennifer Jones graduated from Chestnut Hill College in Philadelphia with a BA in communications with a concentration in journalism and professional writing. She spent time in the field during school doing freelance work for local papers and blogs. After college, she found her passion in creative nonfiction, short essays, and songwriting. She and her partner currently reside in Philadelphia, PA.

photo © Michael Wirtz

Shelly Fisher

Shelly Fisher is a graduate of Syracuse University's SI Newhouse School of Communications, with a minor in psychology. She also holds a master's degree in education from UNC Chapel Hill. While in Chapel Hill she manned a twenty-four-hour crisis intervention line, laying the foundation for her interest in helping others in need and giving back to the community. She is a Philadelphia native and has led multiple small businesses in the area, along with serving on the boards for several educational and charitable organizations. She has been happily married for over thirty years and has three children, three dogs, and a bird.

SELECTED TITLES FROM SHE WRITES PRESS

She Writes Press is an independent publishing company founded to serve women writers everywhere. Visit us at www.shewritespress.com.

All Set for Black, Thanks: A New Look at Mourning by Miriam Weinstein. $16.95, 978-1-63152-109-6. A wry, irreverent take on how we mourn, how we remember, and how we keep our dead with us even as we (sort of) let them go.

Falling Together: How to Find Balance, Joy, and Meaningful Change When Your Life Seems to be Falling Apart by Donna Cardillo. $16.95, 978-1-63152-077-8. A funny, big-hearted self-help memoir that tackles divorce, caregiving, burnout, major illness, fears, and low self-esteem—and explores the renewal that comes when we are able to meet these challenges with courage.

Green Nails and Other Acts of Rebellion: Life After Loss by Elaine Soloway. $16.95, 978-1-63152-919-1. An honest, often humorous account of the joys and pains of caregiving for a loved one with a debilitating illness.

Four Funerals and a Wedding: Resilience in a Time of Grief by Jill Smolowe. $16.95, 978-1-938314-72-8. When journalist Jill Smolowe lost four family members in less than two years, she turned to modern bereavement research for answers—and made some surprising discoveries.

From Sun to Sun: A Hospice Nurse's Reflection on the Art of Dying by Nina Angela McKissock. $16.95, 978-1-63152-808-8. Weary from the fear people have of talking about the process of dying and death, a highly experienced registered nurse takes the reader into the world of twenty-one of her beloved patients as they prepare to leave this earth.

Painting Life: My Creative Journey Through Trauma by Carol K. Walsh. $16.95, 978-1-63152-099-0. Carol Walsh was a psychotherapist working with traumatized clients when she encountered her own traumatic experience; this is the story of how she used creativity and artistic expression to heal, recreate her life, and ultimately thrive.